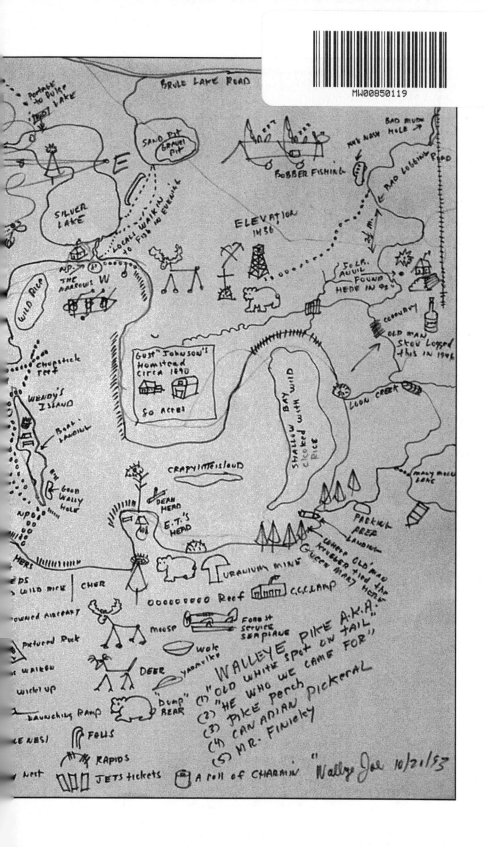

To Mike &
Charlotte,

Enjoy!
Best Regards

Alan

Mar 2023

A Fisherman's Journey

A Lifetime of Angling Adventures from
Northern Wisconsin to Northwest Montana, 1950-2020

by Charles Zucker

sweetgrassbooks
an imprint of Farcountry Press

Dedicated to Shaya, my wonderful wife and fishing partner, and to my brother Joe, with whom I shared fishing adventures for more than fifty years

ISBN 978-1-59152-315-4

© 2022 by Charles Zucker

Inside front cover: *Rice Lake and the surrouding area where I spent so many pleasant hours fishing with my brother Joe, Shaya, Grandpa Ray Kruger and many other intrepid walleye fisherpersons. DRAWING BY "WALLEYE JOE" ZUCKER.*

Inside back cover: *"Fallen Warrior Lake"*
DRAWING BY "WALLEYE JOE" ZUCKER

Design by Steph Lehmann

For more information or to order extra copies of this book
call Farcountry Press toll free at (800) 821-3874
or visit www.farcountrypress.com

s🌱eetgrassbooks
an imprint of Farcountry Press

Produced by Sweetgrass Books
PO Box 5630, Helena, MT 59604; (800) 821-3874; www.sweetgrassbooks.com

Produced and printed in the United States of America

26 25 24 23 22   1 2 3 4 5

Contents

Introduction

Most books about fishing are filled with entertaining stories written by people who have become experts in the piscatorial arts. They are meant to vicariously bring us excitement by sharing stories of lunkers landed or lost.

I certainly am no expert fisherman. I am pretty average to tell the truth, though I have had plenty of good days on the water. And I have had the pleasure of fishing with many expert fisherpersons. This book instead is about my lifelong evolution as a fisherman from my first experiences wetting a line in northern Wisconsin for yellow perch to my latest experiences (but hopefully not my last) fishing for trout in northwest Montana. Like most fishermen, my fishing has evolved over the decades as my life changed and new fishing opportunities opened up for me. My hope is that sharing my experiences with readers I will encourage them to think about their own fishing journey (and hopefully to enjoy some of mine along the way). Fishing is a wonderful sport. But even more wonderful than the fishing itself is the adventures along the way—and especially the people that you meet.

CHAPTER I

The Northern Wisconsin Years: A Kid's Paradise

Summit Lake

My mother, Leah, was born and raised in Antigo, Wisconsin, about 300 miles north of Chicago. After graduating from Antigo high school in 1925, she moved to the Windy City to become a nurse. Soon after, she met my father, Irv, on a blind date at Wrigley Field. I often have thought that the Cubs must have won that day because a few years later they were married. My brother, Joe, was born in 1941 and I followed in 1945. We grew up on the South side of Chicago in a working class and middle class neighborhood typical of post WW II America. Everybody had kids and we knew which family lived in each house for blocks around. We played endlessly during the year—our games changing according to the seasons. Among our favorite were basketball, baseball, and football, golf (hitting balls around in an empty field); hunting garter snakes for our annual snake roundup, catching butterflies, building forts, and constructing our own soap box cars, and playing hide and go seek. Indoors, we played monopoly and read comic books. We also watched our black-and-white TV. People today find it hard to believe that each day we all walked to the local grammar school, Dixon elementary, and then home for lunch where peanut butter and jelly sandwiches that my mother had prepared were waiting for me. Then it was time to walk back to school. Around 3:30 pm school when was out, we all walked home again.

Each summer, the Zucker family loaded up the family vehicle and headed up to northern Wisconsin to visit my mother's extended clan. The trip between Chicago and Antigo took about eight hours since there weren't any interstate highways between the two in the 1950s. The trip, though, was usually a pleasant once we escaped Chicago and reached the rolling hills of Wisconsin dotted with small towns and dairy farms. We would stop in Clintonville for the most delicious ice cream cones imaginable made at the local dairy (my favorite was maple nut), and we always drove through the beautiful Menominee Indian reservation where years later I would fish for trout on the Wolf River.

Antigo in the 1950s was a town of about ten thousand souls (today it has about the same population.) Farming was the backbone of the economy then with some assistance from a growing tourist industry. Most years we probably did not bother to stop to visit but raced ahead the additional seventeen miles on Highway 45 to Summit Lake where our rustic cabin was waiting for us at King's resort. ("Rustic" might be a stretch by today's standards). Our cabin had a kitchen, a living room, a couple of bedrooms, a screened-in porch, and a collection of old furniture. It had a beautiful peek-a-boo view of the lake through the pine and birch trees. The cabin also came with a rowboat (no motor) tied up down at the dock. There was one other resort on the lake (Rasmussen's) and maybe half dozen summer homes. The Wisconsin DNR today describes Summit Lake as 279 acres with a maximum depth of 29 feet. The DNR adds that the resident fish population is composed of "Musky, Panfish, Bass, Northern Pike and Walleye." The DNR's scientific description of the lake does not do it justice. It was, at least, in the 1950s a true gem. The lake water has a reddish tint to it and there is one small island towards the far shoreline. Swimming in the cool waters of Summit Lake was wonderful since the lake drops of gradually and has a sandy bottom.

Beginnings: The Yellow Perch of Summit Lake
There were certainly better fishing lakes around, but Summit Lake was great for kids' fishing. In the 1950s, it was loaded with yellow perch. In the mornings and again in the evenings, my father, my brother, and I would

Summit Lake, Wisconsin, down at the dock, circa 1955. AUTHOR'S COLLECTION.

take the boat out, row down the shore a ways, put a worm on our hook, and toss the line out. Within a minute or so the bobber would go down, we would set the hook, and after a brief tussle a perch would be landed. They were rarely big enough to keep. But who cared? The action was non-stop. It was a great way for both of us to begin our lifelong fishing careers. And once in a blue moon we would get into a school of crappies. Those we kept and ate. I hope to make it one more time to Summit Lake before I hang up my fish-ing gear for good. Things have changed over the last sixty years. Google Earth shows me a lake now ringed with cottages. King's Cabins is long gone. But I bet the perch are still biting.

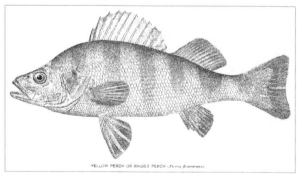

Yellow perch. ILLUSTRATION BY HUGH MCCORMICK SMITH, CIRCA 1896, UNIVERSITY OF WASHINGTON.

The Day of the Muskellunge

One day my brother and I were out fishing Summit Lake on our own. As usual, the perch were biting. My brother, Joe, was reeling one in when something totally unexpected happened. His line stopped dead in the water. Something BIG had grabbed the perch. What could it be? We knew that Summit Lake contained some northern pike and the northern's even more ferocious cousin—the muskellunge. The fish had not swallowed the perch but had it in its mouth as my brother reeled in his line. The monster was now right beside the boat—we could look over the side and see the fish. No doubt about it. It was a huge musky. I remember that musky as being almost as long as our rowboat. What were we to do? We had absolutely no experience in catching something that enormous. And we did not have a net. Lacking any other game plan, we decided we would try to "beach" the fish. In retrospect, this was a crazy idea, but it was all we could think of. So, we began rowing ashore, hoping against hope that the musky would continue to hold on to the perch as we dragged the fish on to the shore. Needless to say, the musky dropped the perch. It was gone! We were heartbroken. Of course, now I know that my brother should have let his line out while we waited for the musky to swallow the perch: Smoked a cigarette (hypothetically speaking) or counted to ten before setting the hook. Almost certainly the musky would have made short work of Joe's tackle, but it would have been exciting to have that beast on the line if only for a minute or two. This was not the last time that we would let a big one get away.

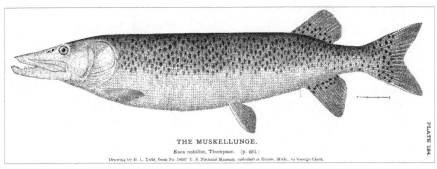

THE MUSKELLUNGE.
Esox nobilior, Thompson. (p. 461.)
Drawing by H. L. Todd, from No 10007 U. S. National Museum, collected at Ecorse, Mich., by George Clark.

Muskellunge. ILLUSTRATION BY GEORGE BROWN GOOD, CIRCA 1884, UNIVERSITY OF WASHINGTON.

Catching the Green Frogs of the Summit Lake Cemetery

Fish were not the only quarry we pursued at Summit Lake. We also went after the big green "racing frogs" that populated the Summit Lake Lakeside Cemetery. At the time, the cemetery was overgrown with weeds. Perhaps that's why the frogs liked to hang out there. I thought at the time that the frogs were perhaps the reincarnation of the people buried there. My brother remembers more details about our frog hunting expeditions than I do, and he was kind enough to send me his recollections. We each carried a two pound coffee can (usually Chase & Sanborns) with a coat hanger attached to it so that we could carry it at our side. We poked and prodded at the weeds with cotton tail stalks hoping to flush the heavily camouflaged frogs from their hiding places. When we caught one, we would place it in the coffee can and put the top back on. With the two of us "beating the bush" we were able to catch a couple dozen frogs a day or two before the Zucker family drove back to the Windy City.

You may ask what did we plan to do with the frogs? Why, my brother planned to sell the slippery amphibians once we got home. He did a lively business peddling most of the frogs to a variety of people: Fishermen planning to use the frogs for bait; kids who wanted to own a frog, etc. Small frogs went for a quarter; medium frogs for fifty cents; and giant frogs for a dollar. Joe remembers that one frog escaped into our basement. I don't know what happened to it. We kept a few, though, for our own devious purposes. "Wayo," one of our many childhood pals, acquired the remaining frogs.

"Wayo" snuck them into the local Walgreens at 87th Street and S. Cottage Grove where he let them go. At the time, we thought this was a hilarious prank. I am not sure how I feel about it now. But, hey, we were kids growing on the South side of Chicago in the 1950s. By the way, the Walgreens is still there.

Northern leopard frog.
RYAN HODNETT, WIKIMEDIA COMMONS.

Social Activities in Northern Wisconsin

My poor mother had to beg and plead with us to take a day off from our kids' activities to visit family and friends in Antigo. Eventually, her pleading would wear us down and off we would go. She had more relatives in and around Antigo that you could shake a stick at. Her favorite was Uncle Art Rammer (her mother's brother). Uncle Art was a railroad engineer, following in the footsteps of my grandfather, Noye Pride, who passed away before I was born. In fact, when we were vacationing at Summit Lake, Uncle Art would blow the locomotive's whistle as the train roared by. Uncle Art had not always been an engineer, though. As a young man, he had worked for a circus as a tightrope walker. The story goes that one day he fell off the rope, injured himself, and decided to pursue a different career.

Those of you who are familiar with Wisconsin know that it has its own unique culture made famous by the "cheese heads." But there is much more to that culture than cheese. In fact, I would rank cheese down on the list behind beer, bratwurst, and the Friday night fish fry at a tavern, restaurant or supper club--another Wisconsin invention. (In the old days, perch were the fish of choice at the fish fry but that has changed sadly because of a huge decline in Lake Michigan's perch population). Of course, you mustn't forget the Green Bay Packers. I have often joked that before being allowed to take up residency in Wisconsin, you have to pass an "entrance" exam: you must demonstrate that you know three recipes for preparing bratwurst using beer and have memorized both the starting offensive and defensive lineup for "the Pack."

Wisconsinites know how to have a good time—maybe in part due to the state's heavy German heritage and maybe in part as a way for compensating for the frequently horrendous weather. Uncle Art passed away when I was still young. I well remember the wake at his house. We were all sad that Uncle Art was gone but that did not stop everybody from having a good time. There was tons of food and libations galore. Alas, the only thing missing from the party was Uncle Art. One year the Zucker family attended a fake wedding organized by our relatives. My brother, who is four years old than I, remembers this affair better me. After consulting with him, what we recollect is that were bride and groom mannequins on the front porch of a cottage somewhere out in the boondocks. I am not sure there was actually a "ceremony" where the couple was "wed" in holy matrimony. But that did not matter. The "wedding" was simply an excuse to have a big party.

When my mother got tired of cooking, our favorite place to eat dinner out was Glenn's High Point, a few minutes' drive north on Highway 45 from our cottage. Glenn himself was usually behind the bar serving drinks when we arrived. He always welcomed our family with a hearty "Hello, folks." The dining room was in the back where you could order a T-bone steak for $1.50 and a whole chicken for $1.25. My brother and I would play the pinball machine while we waited for our food to be cooked. Glenn, an expert fisherman, was always ready to dispense timely tips on where they were biting. Places like Glenn's High Point today are rare.

Fishing Pelican Lake and Post Lake

As we grew older, we were ready to explore other lakes in the area. Two close by were Pelican Lake, famous for its excellent muskie fishing; and Post Lake, a weedy lake filled with northern pike. Pelican Lake is special for me because my grandfather, Noye Pride, owned a cabin on the lake sometime in the early years of the twentieth century. I dearly wish I had a photo of the cabin on Pelican or a photo of Noye with a catch, but I don't. He was an engineer on the Chicago & Northwestern railroad line that ran from northern Wisconsin to the Windy City. The train dropped fishermen off at the lake on its way north from Antigo and then picked them on its way south back to Antigo. In the 1930s, Frank Suick developed the "Suick Muskie Thriller," a big wooden jerk bait, which he first used on Pelican with great success. You can still purchase Suick lures today for about thirty bucks. His family owned Suick's Muskie Bar in Antigo where railroad men and fishermen stopped in to swap stories and have a few drinks. I remember visiting the bar with family members back in the 1950s and 1960s. On one of our visits to Glenn's' High Point, Glenn told us "to try under the wire" at Pelican—a reference to electrical wires running out from shore to an island. Indeed, we did try under the wire one day and were rewarded with a nice catch of assorted panfish. My brother would later catch his first walleyed pike on Pelican, one of thousands of walleyes he would catch over the years. Joe brought the walleye, which he had cleaned and frozen, back to Chicago where we had an unveiling before baking it for dinner. I remember viewing the walleye and being amazed that Joe had caught it. After I graduated from Wisconsin, my brother, my college roommate, Dan, and I made a fall fishing trip to Pelican. We stayed at the old Pelican Lake Hotel, which even at the time was a relic from a bygone era. The floor creaked and the beds were old. A cold front came through and the fishing was slow, but we had a great time anyway. I was surprised to learn that the Pelican Lake Hotel is still in business today. It has been totally refurbished and is now rented out for marriages, family reunions, and the like. Today you can rent out the entire 9,500-square-foot hotel, which can accommodate up to 200 guests. But Post Lake is where we would concentrate our efforts as we entered our late teenage years and on into our early twenties.

There was nothing exceptional about the toothy northerns that inhabited the 379 acres of Lower Post Lake in the 1960s. The lake is shallow with a maximum depth of about nine feet and weedy—perfect habitat for old *Esox lucius*. The pike we were to catch on many trips to the lake perhaps averaged three pounds and I don't think we ever caught one that weighed more than six pounds. But to boys who had grown up in Chicago, fishing for Post Lake's northerns was high adventure. We would rent a cabin on the lake for four or five days in June. Sometimes one of my brother's friends, George, would join us. We would buy our bait—big sucker minnows—at Bob Marine's tackle shop located a few miles from the lake. Bob, in fact, taught me a simple knot to tie, which I still use today while fly fishing. No self-respecting fly fisherman would ever use this knot, but the truth is that I am a total klutz when it comes to tying knots. Using Bob's knot, I can tie a fly onto to my line in less than a minute. Today, this gives me an advantage when fishing for trout in crowded circumstances. I have seen trout fisherman on the Guadalupe River in Texas spend ten minutes or more on the bank tying a textbook knot. There's an old adage in fishing:

The more time your line is in the water, the better the odds are that you will catch a fish. Have I lost any fish because of my unconventional knot? Perhaps a few but not many.

Our *modus operandi* when fishing for Post Lake northerns was to the minnow three to four feet below the bobber. Then we would sit and wait. And wait. If we were lucky, the northerns would be hungry. Suddenly one of our bobbers would disappear from the surface of the lake and begin moving at a rapid clip away from the boat. Our hearts would be in our mouths. Who knew how large the beast might be that had grabbed the minnow? With northerns—like the muskellunge—the fisherman has to wait for the fish to swallow the bait. But how long does one wait? That is the question. If the fisherman strikes too soon, the fish will get away. But there is also danger in waiting too long. So, timing is everything. If the one of us who had the strike hit it just right, a short but exciting tussle would take place before the fish was landed. Northerns, though, can be persnickety. Many days we struck out—especially when the conditions were not favorable. Northerns, like many game fish, do not like sunny weather. Bluebird skies and a north wind usually left us fishless. Years later in the late 1970s when my wife and I were living in Waukesha, Wisconsin, we would make several more trips to Post Lake. It was still wonderful place and the northerns were still abundant. But it has now been more than thirty years since I fished Post Lake, so I am not sure how good the fishing is today. Maybe when I make that final trip to Summit Lake, I will try my luck at Post Lake as well.

Northern pike. ILLUSTRATION BY GEORGE BROWN GOOD, CIRCA 1884, UNIVERSITY OF WASHINGTON.

The Trout of the Peshtigo and Wolf Rivers

As children and then teenagers, my brother and I never fished for trout on our own in northern Wisconsin. The trout were certainly there. Buy trying to catch a trout was a whole different cup of tea. Occasionally, though, the Antigo relatives would take us to a trout pond back in the woods. One day one dad lost a big rainbow at one of these ponds. Well, actually he did successfully land the rainbow. But then disaster struck. He got so excited by his catch that he ran to tell us about it. It took only a few seconds for the fish to flop from the shore back into the pond. It was gone. My dad was heartbroken. Moral of the story: Never leave your catch unattended on the shore.

After graduating from the University of Wisconsin in 1966, I entered the Ph.D. program in history at Northwestern University in Evanston, Illinois. I was fortunate to have two graduate school buddies who loved to fish. The first was Don Doyle. He was an experienced trout fisherman having grown up in northern California. After much discussion, Don convinced me one spring that we should head up to head up to northern Wisconsin to fish the Peshtigo River. If memory serves, we had spinning lures and maybe were dangling a piece of worm off the end of the hook. Shortly after beginning to fish, I had a strike. What could it possibly be? I was puzzled. Don yelled to me, "It's a trout." I was thunderstruck. One could actually catch a trout in a river! We spent a few days catching some trout on the Peshtigo and some of its tributaries. On the second or third day of our trip, we met another intrepid trout fisherman, Chief Oshkosh of the Menominee Indians. The chief proved to be more than willing to show Don and me some his favorite spots, and we spent many pleasant hours conversing with him. On the negative side of the ledger, in all my years of fishing, this was only time I ever had anyone pull a gun on me. I was rounding the bend of a creek when I saw a man standing on the shore. He was pointing a pistol at me. "This is private property," he said. "Turn around and leave." I am not sure the creek itself was private property, but I was not about to argue with him. Still makes me mad after all these years.

The Peshtigo, though, was not my only experience fishing for trout in northern Wisconsin. A few years after receiving my Ph.D. in history from Northwestern, I landed a job at Carroll College (now Carroll University) located in Waukesha, Wisconsin, just outside of Milwaukee. As an assistant professor, I found even less time to fish than I had as a graduate student. But, again, I was still up for an occasional fishing trip. My wife's college roommate, Sandy, loved to fish—in fact, she still does. So, my wife, Shaya, Sandy, her first husband, Mike, and I headed up to camp and fish for trout in a stretch of the Wolf River actually located inside the Menominee Indian Reservation. At the time you could pay the Menominee a small fee for camping and fishing inside the reservation. My trout fishing gear remained basic. I believe that I actually owned some hip waders, though it would be more many years until I owned such fancy gear as chest waders, a fishing vest, and wading staff.

Expert fishermen know that the best fishing is always to be found far away from the place where you begin. If it's lake fishing you are doing, it's obligatory to race off in your motor boat to the opposite side of the lake; if it's in the ocean, why, then, the best fishing is at least forty miles off shore; and if it's in a river, the fish are sure to be biting best at a minimum of one mile or two upstream or downstream. This was my operational theory, in any case, one morning on the Wolf as we set out to fish. Shaya and Sandy decided to stay put at the campsite right on the shore of the Wolf. I told the them they would never catch a trout sitting there—that, based on my vast experience, you had to trudge up the river tripping over rocks and boulders for a long way before you could even think about catching a trout. Well, I am sure you know how things turned out. Mike and I managed to fall in the Wolf several times and did not even get a bite. When we returned to camp, Shaya and Sandy had a dandy catch of trout that they had caught sitting on a rock fifty feet from our tents. That happened over forty years ago, but I still hear about it today from the ladies.

The first time I ever saw a master fly fisherman at work was on the Wolf. It was at dusk and we were back in camp. A young man waded out into the river and climbed up on a rock. He began casting his line with a beautiful fluid motion and, bang, within a few minutes he had a big rainbow on the line. He landed the fish and then two or three more before it became too dark to fish. I was in awe. And like so many fishing memories, the image of him standing on the rock catching those trout is still vivid in my mind. I made a mental note to try fly fishing someday, but it would be many years before I would cast my first fly.

Coho Salmon and Carp

My second fishing buddy while I was in graduate school at Northwestern was John Reiger. John grew up in New York and Miami in a family of avid fishers and hunters. His research interest at Northwestern was in the history of conservation in America. In 1975, a revised version of his dissertation, *American Sportsmen and the Origins of Conservation,* was published. Many years later, he authored a second book, *Escaping Into Nature,* a wonderful highly personal account of the importance of hunting and fishing in coping with a traumatic childhood.

John and I embarked on three fishing adventures together while we were in graduate school. After we received our Ph.D.s, we went our separate ways. It was not until I sent in a brief blurb to the NU History Department's online newsletter in 2019 that I heard again from John. We have been in touch many times since then and chatting on the Internet has helped me refresh my memory about our fishing adventures. The first adventure was fishing for Coho Salmon in Lake Michigan. Coho were first stocked in Lake Michigan in 1966, which fortuitously was the same year that we both entered graduate school at Northwestern. Also fortuitous is the fact that Northwestern is located on the shore of Lake Michigan. The stocking was successful and within a few years large schools of cohos were roaming the waters of Lake Michigan. So, one day we packed our fishing gear into a leaky canoe and ventured out into the lake. Neither of us can remember who's canoe it was or where we got it. John remembers that we trolled for the cohos right off of Lake Shore Drive with cars whizzing by and skyscrapers looming behind us. I was in the bow and John was in the back. We synchronized our paddling on opposite sides of the canoe. He also remembers trolling a Mepps spinning lure; I do not remember what lure I used. We had great action. With the space of a few hours we had caught several cohos in the two-pound category. We each kept three and released several. But the waves were getting rougher and the canoe was still leaking, so we headed back to shore. Amazingly, John has a photo of me my catch. Those were not the only salmon that I caught during my Northwestern years. Shaya and I also caught some fishing from shore on the NU campus.

Coho salmon. TIMOTHY KNEPP, U.S. FISH AND WILDLIFE SERVICE.

The second adventure is somewhat embarrassing for two "purist" fisherpersons to admit to: We went snagging for carp in the suburb of Winnetka's power plant warm water discharge outlet on the shore of Lake Michigan. Now, if you are indeed a true purist, you may not know what the art of "snagging" for fish entails. It's pretty simple actually. All you need to do is make a trip to your local sporting goods store to purchase a bunch of large treble hooks. When you arrive at the appointed place to begin snagging, you tie a treble hook on the end of your line, cast the line out into the water, and begin to reel it in at a furious pace. If you are lucky, your treble hook will lodge somewhere in the body of the hapless fish and the fight will be on. Sporting? Perhaps not. Fun? Definitely, yes, when the quarry is very large carp. Now here's the thing about our second fishing adventure. Both of us remember that after a terrific battle we each pulled in a gigantic carp. I know I caught one that weighed around twenty pounds. But John also has photos of this adventure. What they show is the two of us posing with mediocre sized carp. What happened to the photos of the lunkers, we do not know. Okay, I know what you are thinking: We never caught those big carp. You believe we that the fish we did catch have grown in our imaginations over the years. But we are convinced that is not the case. Is snagging legal? The answer is in most instances is that it is not; but in some case it is. In northwestern Montana, for example, there's a run of spawning Kokanee Salmon up the Tobacco River near the town of Eureka where it's legal to snag for them. Have I ever snagged for Kokanee? No, but Shaya and I have watched fisherpersons snag for them on the Tobacco. It's food for the table.

The common carp, by the way, is not native to North America. Carp were brought here from Europe and stocked intensively by the U.S. Commission of Fish and Fisheries in the late nineteenth century. Although they were prized in Europe, they soon became despised in the United States. Sportsmen blamed them for despoiling the waters of native game fish. However, in recent years, the common carp has made something of a comeback—they are now eagerly pursued by many fly fishers. Go figure.

Me with a carp I snagged on Lake Michigan circa 1968-1970.
AUTHOR'S COLLECTION.

Our third expedition was to Post Lake to fish for Northern pike. To be honest, I had totally forgotten about this trip—perhaps because the fishing was bad. But we managed to catch a few, and John has a photo he provided for me with him and a northern.

CHAPTER II

Fishing the Tar Heel State and Meeting the Extended Family

Moving to Fayetteville

My first teaching job out of graduate school was at Fayetteville State University in North Carolina. In fact, I first found out about the job opening when I returned from a fishing trip to Minnesota towards the end of my graduate school days at Northwestern. The History Department secretary informed me that the president of Fayetteville State had called looking for a likely candidate to fill an opening at the university. My name popped up at the head of the list because the Fayetteville State is a historically black university and my research in graduate school focused on the history of race relations in the United States. So, I flew down to Fayetteville in 1970 to interview for the job, which was offered to me a week or so later. I accepted the offer and in the summer of 1970 we moved to Fayetteville—about six months after Shaya and I were married.

To be honest, Fayetteville was not a great place to live in the early 1970s. But our move to North Carolina had one saving grace. Shaya's family hails from the Tar Heel State. Her mother's extended family lives in the area around Belhaven, a town of about 1,600 located on the Pungo River in eastern NC. In those days, it was about a three-and-a-half hour drive from Fayetteville to Belhaven. As far as we can tell, Shaya's ancestors got off the boat several hundred years ago somewhere in North Carolina; most of them apparently never moved far away from where they had landed. So, every two or three weeks, we would drive pack up the Chevrolet Townsmen station wagon and make the drive from Fayetteville to Belhaven to visit. Years before, Herbert, my father-in-law and Ginger, my mother-in-law, had purchased a small cottage, "Birdsong," on about five acres of land outside of Belhaven. So, we even had a place to stay. Until I married into the Gornstein family, I did not have any relatives who hailed from the South. It was new experience for me.

I remember meeting the extended family on my first visit to the farm. Shaya's grandparents, aunts, uncles, and countless cousins were among the most welcoming people I had ever met. For the moment I arrived, I was a member of the family. There was only one problem: I had trouble understanding them. This area of North Carolina back in the 1970s had its own unique dialect: One that some linguists believe is closely patterned after the original English settlers. Not too long after I arrived on my first visit, one of Shaya's uncles, Laurie (better known as "Boodle") asked me to go for a ride with him and a friend in his pickup truck. I was able to understand that I had been asked to go along with him. Of course, I accepted, and off we went. During this hour long ride, I was able to understand that Boodle and his friends were talking mostly about fishing nets. But that was about all I could understand. It was very much like if I had had one semester of French and found myself in Paris. Naturally, after several visits, I was able to understand them perfectly.

Grandpa and Grandma Jordan lived on about a twenty-acre farm located on North Creek, which flows into the Pamlico River. Before he retired, Grandpa made his living raising tobacco and doing some commercial fishing. In fact, as a girl, Shaya remembers going fishing with him on his sailboat. During the two years that we lived in Fayetteville, four out of five of Shaya's uncles still lived in the area: In addition to Laurie, there was George, David, and Joe: They all made their living as commercial fishermen taking their boats out into the Pamlico Sound. They hauled nets for fish and oysters and set pots for crabs. Guess what they did on their day off? They went fishing, of course. This usually involved taking a cane pole down to the dock on the farm and still fishing for whatever was biting. Since North Creek contained brackish water, one could expect to catch a variety of both fresh and saltwater fish. If the tide were in, why, you might land some croakers, mullet, flounder or a speckled trout; if the tide were out, you might catch some pumpkinseed sunfish, white perch, and the occasional largemouth bass. And, of course, there were always the ever-present eels. (Striped bass are the big gamefish in the area, but you need a big powerboat to pursue them.)

Fishing Up the Guts

Of course, we took my twelve-foot Montgomery Ward SeaKing aluminum boat and our five-and-a-half horsepower Johnson outboard (on loan from Herbert) with us on our trips to the farm. This was also a different kind of fishing from what I had previously experienced. If you were to go on Google Earth and type in "North Creek" or "Pungo River," you would discover that this area of North Carolina is a maze of creeks and rivers. One of the favorite ways for locals to fish is to take a boat up a "gut." There are many definitions of the word "gut" and one of them is a "narrow passage or strait." And that's a pretty good description of what "guts" are in this neck of the woods: Creeks averaging perhaps twenty feet wide and a few hundred feet long that flow into a larger body of water. So, the fisherpersons would take a boat out from a dock and head for a gut. Once you reached one, you would cut the motor (if you had one) and row up the gut until you found a likely spot and began fishing. Guts are productive places to catch a variety of fish because there is lots of cover provided by trees and stumps in the water. So, if you were lucky you might catch a mess of sunfish or croakers.

There was only one problem in fishing these guts: Snakes. This area of North Carolina is snake heaven. The most dangerous of the local snake population is the cottonmouth water moccasin (*Agkistrodon piscivorus*). Shortly after Shaya and I were married, we took a brief vacation to Post Lake. Of course, I had been there many times, but she had not. We arrived at our cabin just as the sun was setting. I was eager for her to see the lake;

so, I asked her to walk down the path to the dock with me. But she adamantly refused to go. All my pleading was in vain. Shaya would not walk down to the dock. I was baffled. After visiting Grandpa and Grandma Jordan, a light bulb went on in my head. "Ah hah!" I thought to myself. "After spending summer vacations down on the farm with her parents, she has become terrified of snakes."

And with good reason. You had to be careful what you were doing whether you were walking or in a boat. Shaya was out fishing with her Mom one day on North Creek and the two had just rowed the old wooden fishing boat up the gut that's located right next to the farm. Shaya spied a large tire on the shore and said to her Mom, "What's that tire doing on the shore? Somebody must have tossed it there." Of course, you may be able to guess what happened next. The tire started moving. I had a similar encounter. I was casting spinning lures when my lure got caught on a tree stump in the water. I rowed over to the stump to the free the lure and had just reached out to grab it when something caught my eye: An enormous cottonmouth was wrapped around the stump. That could have been a disaster. Had I not seen the cottonmouth at the last second, I almost certainly would have been bitten.

Cottonmouth. PETER PAPLANUS, WIKIMEDIA COMMONS.

In fact, one of the few hunting experience in my life took place on that same gut next to the farm. I decided to try my luck one day from the dilapidated dock on the gut. In the old days, this dock had been used to tie up the family's forty-foot-long commercial fishing boats. In recent years, though, they had moved their boats to better locations. However, the gut had become the final resting place for a few relics that were no longer in use. They were partially sunk in about six feet of water. It was Grandpa Jordan's practice to throw small fish he had caught into the hold of one these boats where they could grow to a larger size. In this way, he always had a supply of fish on hand that he could "harvest." When I walked out onto the dock and spied the water around me, I could see at least a half-dozen cottonmouths. Some were lounging in the old bailing wire that had once been crab pots, while others were reposing on either one of the old boats or hanging out on shore. I decided against making any casts. Instead, I walked calmly back to the farmhouse to report to Grandma Jordan what I had scene. She said to me, "Well, take Grandpa's rifle and I will give you some shells to shoot the snakes."

So, a few minutes later, the Great White Hunter returned to the dock to dispatch the cottonmouths. Now, Grandpa's old .22-caliber rifle was a bit unusual because the barrel was crooked. That was going to make hitting the snakes more challenging. Grandma had given me about a half dozen shells loaded with .22 shot, which I had placed in the pocket of my short sleeve shirt. Big mistake. When I arrived at the appointed destination, I crouched down on my left knee on the dock. As I was beginning to take aim at one of the snakes before loading the rifle, the shells fell out of my pocket and, kerplunk, rolled into the drink. My mouth fell open. Now what was I going to do? I could just hear all the relatives having a good laugh at my expense: City slicker Charles drops all of his shells in the gut and snakes get away! I seriously considered telling a fib to Grandma—that I had shot the snakes and they were all dead. But what if someone went down there and one of the cottonmouths bit them? In the end, I walked back to the farmhouse to report to Grandma what had happened and to ask for more shells. I was mightily embarrassed. Grandma, to her credit, did not say anything but her body language said everything. She fetched more shells for me. I walked down to the dock again. This time I was careful not to drop the shells. And even with the curved rifle barrel, I was able to kill several of the cottonmouths. You know, I don't know if I did any fishing at the dock that day after the snake hunt. It's happened a long time ago.

I fished with several of Shaya's relatives over the two years we lived in North Carolina. Many times it involved just taking some frozen shrimp for bait from grandma's freezer down to the dock where we try our luck for whatever was biting. On other occasions, I might venture out into North Creek or the Pamlico River with one of the cousins or uncles. I remember one chilly autumn day in particular when Uncle Joe and I went fishing in the SeaKing. Scudding clouds were blowing across the sky as I maneuvered the Sea King up North Creek for a mile or two before we took shelter in a small bay. We did not really expect to catch much. To our surprise, the most beautiful pumpkinseed sunfish I have ever seen had schooled up in the bay. I caught a dozen or so on my spinning rods using worms for bait. I forget what kind of gear Uncle Joe used, but he caught a bunch of them too. They must have weighed close to a pound each. Naturally, we took them back to the farm where grandma cooked them for supper. My favorite fishing pal during my two years in North Carolina was Shaya's first cousin, Dennis. We went on numerous expeditions together. At the time, Dennis was a strapping young man who, if memory serves, was about six feet two inches tall and as strong as an ox. Tragically, a few years after we left Fayetteville, he was diagnosed with cancer. Dennis did not make it. I often still think about him.

Brother Joe Comes to Visit

My brother, who had moved from Minneapolis to New York City by this time to pursue his art career, also visited for four or five days one spring to fish. We spent a lot of casting for bass on North Creek and on the Pamlico River but did not have much luck. I think the reason for why the fishing was not any better for bass by the time I arrived in North Carolina had to do with pollution. Years before, a phosphate plant was built near the tiny town of Bayview on the Pamlico River. The Aurora mine is the largest integrated phosphate mining and chemical plant in the world. After the mining plant went into operation, the fishing went downhill. Of course, there were other reasons involved too. The spread of farming in the area meant that fertilizer used for crops was getting into the watershed. Sigh.

Joe and I went on several memorable adventures. One of the uncles (I don't remember which one) told me several times to try our luck on the "The Frying Pan," a body of water that is shaped like—guess what—a frying pond, that is part of the Alligator River in deep eastern North Carolina. The152,000-acre Alligator River National Wildlife Refuge was created in 1984 (over a decade after we left Fayetteville) to preserve and protect the unique wetland habitat. It's one of the premier strongholds of the American black bear on the Eastern seaboard and is also is home to a wide variety of birds and other critters. That Joe and I managed to find the "frying pan" and launch the SeaKing in itself was quite a feat. In all of the places that I have fished in my lifetime, I consider this to be one of the most remote. A wonderful article by Ed Wall in the Sun Journal (New Bern, NC, April 24, 2014), "The Alligator is a springtime treat," describes fishing on the river for bass and bream in more recent times. In the spring, "largemouth bass congregate in the shallows, many of them thick with Eurasian Milfoil" where they remain foraging for baitfish until midsummer," he writes. Tree stumps are another popular place for a fisherperson to try his or her luck. The fishing, though, "can, by turns, be as good or challenging " as any in that part of the country. "The action can from red-hot to stone-cold with the suddenness of someone turning off a switch." Alas, on the day that Joe and I fished the "frying pan" the action was pretty stone cold. Joe did manage to catch a ten-pound catfish. I don't remember whether we kept it or not. It would not be fair to the "Frying Pan" if I did not admit that we were pretty clueless as to how to fish this kind of water. A more experienced angle might have done better.

Our second big adventure was a trip to fish Lake Mattamuskeet. If you have never been to this lake, I can only say that it is about as different as the lakes that brother Joe and I were used to fishing as one could imagine.

21

Lake Mattamuskeet, located in a remote area of Hyde County, is North Carolina's largest natural lake. It is eighteen miles long and seven miles wide, covering 40 thousand acres. In addition, miles of canals are available for shore fishermen. What is most strange about this lake is its depth: The whole shebang is only two to three feet deep! The U.S Fish & Wildlife Service states that the favorite species to catch are largemouth bass, white perch, crappie, sunfish, and blue crabs.

Bryan Mims describes the fascinating history of this lake in an article in *Our State* (April 2014) entitled, "The Sleeping Giant of Lake Mattamuskeet." In the early twentieth century, locals came up with a plan to drain the lake so that the rich land lying beneath it could be used for farming. In 1915, a pumping station was constructed to accomplish that end, and indeed the lake was drained several times over the next few decades. When the project was abandoned because it proved to be too costly to keep the lake dry, the old pumping station was turned into a

Rear view of Mattamuskeet Lodge. DAVID MIMS, WIKIMEDIA COMMONS.

grand lodge, sporting a garnet-red tile roof and a blue-and-white twelve-story observation tower. Mattamuskeet Lodge was once a mecca for goose hunters. But when the goose population plummeted, the lodge closed to guests in 1974. Hunters, though, were not the only guests at the lodge. Mims notes that Rachel Carson once stayed there while writing for the U.S. Fish and Wildlife Service. Shaya and I were living in Fayetteville when the lodge was still open, and I remember visiting it with her. The place struck me at the time as eerie. Bird watchers have now replaced hunters at Lake Mattamuskeet. More than 240 bird species fill the air around the lake—including snow geese, great blue herons, egrets, and several species of ducks. The lake's most famous feathered visitors, though, are the magnificent tundra swans that fly in from the Arctic by the thousands to spend the winter.

But back to fishing. Joe and I launched the SeaKing from one of the canals and began exploring this vast lake. But where to go with 40,000 acres to fish? We spent several hours casting our spinning lures but without much success. It was spring and it turned out that the bass were spawning. I don't remember exactly why we decided to explore a shallow pond connected to the main lake. What I do remember is pulling the boat up on shore and walking over a small rise to see if there were any fish in the pond. When I looked down into the water, I was agape: Dozens of big bass (or "chubs" as the locals call them) were swimming around. We rushed back to the boat for our rods and began casting. One rushed across the pond and smashed my lure. I caught that one and then another and Joe caught several too. Between the two of us we landed about a half-dozen bass in the four-pound category. But then we decided to stop fishing and return to the boat. Can you guess why we quit? Because the area was infested with our "old friend"—the cottonmouth water moccasin! We literally had to watch every step we took. We motored back across the lake to the spot where we had put in and headed back to "Birdsong" where we enjoyed a dinner of largemouth bass. I remember discussing with Joe whether we should head back to the same spot in the morning, but in the end we decided against it. There were two reasons we opted not to return: First, we were terrified of

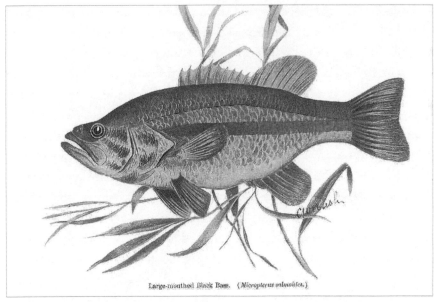

Large-mouthed Black Bass. (*Micropterus salmoides.*)

Largemouth bass. ILLUSTRATION BY C.W. NASH, CIRCA 1908, WIKIMEDIA COMMONS.

the moccasins and, second, we had reservations about catching spawning bass. I am not sure which reason weighed more heavily on us.

Our last adventure was to the spectacularly beautiful Outer Banks, a 200-mile-long string of barrier islands off of the coast of North Carolina and Virginia. Much of the Outer Banks is protected by the Cape Hatteras National Seashore established in 1937. It's about a hundred-mile, two-hour drive, from Belhaven to the Outer Banks. So, we planned to stay overnight at one of the local motels. We took Highway 264 through some of the most remote areas of the United States that one could find back then, passing through towns like Swanquarter, Engelhard, and Stumpy Point. At Manns Harbor, we turned off onto Highway 64, traveled across Croatan Sound to Roanoke Island, and finally to the Outer Banks where we connected to Highway 12. Although it's been almost fifty years, I am sure that we then headed towards Oregon Inlet—a mecca for salt-water fishing. Today, it's home to the Oregon Inlet Fishing Center which boasts that it has the "largest and most modern charter boat fishing fleet on the eastern seaboard." So, if its Blue Marlin, Sailfish, Yellowfin Tuna, Wahoo or any number of other hard fighting salt water species that you may be after, this is the place for you to go. Back in the day, though, brother Joe and I had much more modest ambitions. We did not have the bread to hire a charter boat to take us out onto the deep blue sea. We planned to do some surfcasting from shore with rods that we had borrowed from Herbert. After reaching Oregon Inlet, we stopped in a tackle store to buy some bait and headed down the coastline to find a likely spot to fish. Frankly, it was once again one of those situations where I did not expect to catch anything. I was about to be surprised. About an hour after we arrived, the line went zipping off my reel. Something big had grabbed the bait. I set the hook and after about a ten-minute tussle brought to shore a ten-pound bluefish. We caught two more ten pounders that day. The next morning, we had to head back to Birdsong. We had bluefish for dinner that night. By the way, Joe would return to Oregon Inlet years later to do some deep-sea fishing with a friend from New York. After a battle that lasted over an hour, Joe landed a marlin that weighed over 400 pounds!

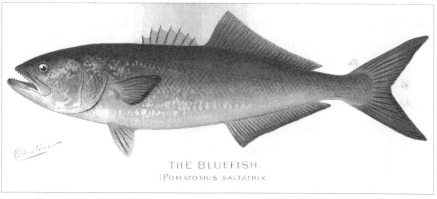

THE BLUEFISH.
[POMATOMUS SALTATRIX]

Bluefish. ILLUSTRATION FROM NEW YORK STATE COMMISSIONERS OF FISHERIES, GAME AND FORESTS, CIRCA 1900, UNIVERSITY OF WASHINGTON.

Life and Times in Eastern North Carolina in the 1970s

In many ways, Shaya and I shared similar backgrounds. My father, Irving, and Shaya's dad, Herbert, were both Jews who grew up in big cities. They both married Gentile women who were raised in what were then remote rural areas: My mother, Leah, in northern Wisconsin and Shaya's mother, Ginger, in eastern North Carolina. Both mothers converted to Judaism after they were married. The fact that Shaya and I were raised in the Jewish religion, though, did not stop our families from celebrating Christmas. We had "Hanukkah bushes" and opened presents on Christmas Day. The Gentile relatives on my side of the family were both Protestants and Catholics; on Shaya's side of the family, they were Protestants of various denominations such as Free Will Baptists and Methodists. We also had in common that the Christian relatives on both sides of the family were welcoming to their new Jewish relatives. The first time Herbert visited the family in North Carolina after he and Ginger were married, Grandpa Jordan reached out to the small Jewish community in the area and invited a Jewish person to visit the farm after Herbert arrived so that he would feel more at home. And a story I heard recounted many times when I was growing up had to do with a roadhouse somewhere outside of Antigo that did not welcome Jews on the premises. It so happened that one of my mother's cousins happened to be the local sheriff at the time. The sheriff and my dad drove out to the roadhouse together in the squad car one evening and that was the end of that.

Both of our families also shared a passion for hunting and fishing. My grandfather, Noye Pride, who passed away before I was born was both an avid hunter and fisherman. He was an engineer for many years on the Milwaukee Line traveling from the far reaches of northern Wisconsin to Chicago. Legend had it that he every so often he would stop the train in a prime location so that he could get off and fish. I treasure a photograph I have of my grandfather after a successful deer hunt with some of his hunting buddies. When I was growing up, most of the relatives in northern Wisconsin fished and many of them were hunters. As I have already mentioned, Shaya's countless relatives in eastern North Carolina spent much of their time fishing year round and in the fall they went hunting for deer. I am not a hunter, so I can't so much about hunting in eastern North Carolina. I do love one story that Uncle Raymond told us about hunting. Raymond was one relative who had flown the coop. He had moved to northern Ohio as a young man because the job opportunities were better there. Of all Shaya's uncles, I think he was my favorite. Raymond was a bow hunter. He had been out hunting for deer for several days without any luck whatsoever. Finally, his big chance came. He was walking towards a fence and was about to pass through the gate, when a thundering herd of deer ran towards him. He was so surprised that he froze—never got a shot off. Shaya and I visited Raymond and his wife, Glow, in Ohio on our way back from North Carolina to Chicago one year. He lived very close to Lake Erie, so naturally he took us out fishing in his boat. The water was rough, and Raymond must have been doing close to thirty miles an hour as we sped towards one of his favorite spots. I remember we caught some nice walleyes, but I don't think my kidneys have been the same since.

Food is central to most cultures and that is certainly true of the culture of eastern North Carolina. Shaya's uncles often still docked their boats at the farm on North Creek where they would unload their catch. The oysters were big and plentiful back in the 1970s. And they were delicious raw or cooked when they were fresh off of the boat. Grandpa Jordan was a master at shucking oysters. The only problem was that he ate about two oysters out of every three he shucked. I believe the best Thanksgiving dinner that I ever had was one prepared by grandma Jordan. The oyster stuffing was to die for. And then were the crabs. I remember one day when one of the uncles gave Herbert a whole pale full of crabs just unloaded from the fishing boat. Back at Birdsong, we steamed the crabs and then ate them all. The fish the caught on North Creek were good too. Grandma would fry them in oil. Mighty tasty but not very healthy. In fact, frying fish and other treasures of the sea was a way of life in eastern North Carolina. I am sure it contributed to health problems that many men developed then. The other gastronomical delight that I learned to love during my two years in North Carolina was the vinegar-based barbecue. It's totally different than the ketchup-based barbecue that we enjoy in Texas.

Sadly, Grandpa Jordan passed away during our second year in Fayetteville. Shaya and I had spent a wonderful weekend visiting the farm and were on our way home when an ambulance sped by us going the other way. As it passed by us, we wondered who might have fallen ill. When we arrived back in Fayetteville, we received a call from Shaya's dad informing us that Grandpa Jordan had died. Shaya remembers that I went fishing with him the day before he departed this world. I don't remember that, but I would like to think that I did. Later, we learned the details of what had happened. In his later years, grandpa had become something of a holy roller. He belonged to one of

Grandma Jordan, Ginger, and me in front of the farmhouse on North Creek, circa 1973. AUTHOR'S COLLECTION.

the many small churches that dot the countryside in this area of North Carolina. He loved to sing hymns and was up in the front of the church belting out "Telephone to Glory" when, according to eyewitnesses, a beatific look came into his eye and he "fell out." Apparently, the call was answered. One of my great disappointments is that Shaya and I did not record him singing while we lived in North Carolina. We attended his funeral, which struck us as something from a by-gone era. Hundreds of people came from miles around and, of course, afterwards there "was food on the grounds." Grandma lived for many more years in her beloved farmhouse on North Creek before going to a nursing home where so passed away well into her 90s. Shaya's mom and dad are buried in the same family cemetery as grandpa and grandma and many other members of the extended clan. The deal that Ginger struck with Herbert was "I will live with you in the North in this life if you will be buried with me in North Carolina." He lived up to the bargain.

In my second year at Fayetteville State, I finished my doctorate and was offered a teaching position at Carroll College. We both thought long and hard about staying but in the end decided that life in Fayetteville left a lot to be desired. I often think that if Fayetteville State had been located in the Raleigh-Durham area, we would have stayed. Several years ago, after visiting good friends in Raleigh-Durham, Shaya and I made one last trip to the Belhaven area to visit relatives. Shaya took with her several photographs of family ancestors that we had inherited from her mother and gifted them out to the family members. We had a wonderful time visiting but, of course, it was not the same. Birdsong has been demolished and the five acres of land on which it sat is totally overgrown. We did not even visit the farm on North Creek where one of Shaya's cousins now lives with her family. It would have been too sad.

CHAPTER III

The Minnesota Years: Pursuing Walleyes, Smallmouth Bass, Northern Pike and Brook Trout

The North Shore of Minnesota

In 1966, my brother received his master's degree from the Art Institute of Chicago and moved to Minneapolis to begin his career as a faculty member at the Minneapolis College of Art and Design. In Minneapolis, he met his first wife, Susan, who had been raised by her grandparents on the north shore of Lake Superior in the small town of Tofte. In fact, Susan's grandfather, Ray, was a legendary fishing guide who owned and operated the North Shore Lodge. The lodge was a classic northwoods establishment. It had a rustic main lodge where you could rent a room for about five dollars per night and for an extra few bucks you got your meals. Joe and I stayed in the lodge many times. If you had some more money to spend, you could spurge for a cabin, which rented for about twenty dollars per night. And, of course, Ray guided. Many of his clients were state legislators since he worked for years in the off-season as the Secretary of the Minnesota Senate. After meeting Susan, it did not take Joe long to discover the wonders of walleye and brook trout fishing in the area.

The north shore of Minnesota in the late 1960s was not exactly a howling wilderness but it was pretty darned close to it. In those days, the eighty-mile ride from Duluth up to Tofte took more than two hours as you wound your way along Highway 61 through the small towns of Two Harbors, Beaver Bay, Silver Bay, and Schroeder before arriving at the lodge. Today, it's an easy drive on the Interstate. Grandpa Kreuger and a few other adventurous souls like the legendary Justine Kerfoot had opened up the vast country to tourism in the 1950s. The Minnesota lakes and rivers I was to fish are located in the Superior National Forest (established in 1909) between the border of the United States and Canada and the north shore of Lake Superior. It falls under the administration of the USDA Forest Service and comprises over 6,000 square miles. To put this in perspective, the Superior National Forest has more square miles than the state of Connecticut. About one quarter of it is set aside as the Boundary Waters Canoe Area (BWCA). The SNF waters include some 2,000 lakes and rivers, more than 1,300 miles of cold water streams, and 950 miles of warm water streams. A map of the area shows that rivers and portages connect hundreds of these lakes. To say that one could spend several lifetimes exploring these lakes and rivers would be an understatement.

Although I will always have a fond place in my heart for fishing northern Wisconsin, the lakes and rivers of northeastern Minnesota represented—to use a bridge term—a jump shift in terms of the fishing experience.

Especially in the early years of my trips to the area, the fishing for walleyes, brook trout, smallmouth bass and northerns was superb. This does not mean that they were always easy to catch. We were often skunked when the conditions were not favorable or the fish for reasons they only knew just refused to bite. For those readers who have not fished for the walleye, I think an apt description of the sport to say is that it resembles hunting. Walleyes are preeminently school fish. They like to hang out in rocks and prefer to feed on the shore on which the wind is blowing. When you find one, you are likely to find many. The trick, of course, is to find that first walleye in big lakes that are filled with structure. Unlike a lot of other fresh water sport fishing, calm conditions spell disaster for the walleye fisherman. The more the wind is howling, the better. And, of course, cloudy conditions are better than bright sunshine.

Our modus operandi for walleye fishing was to stop at the bait store on the way to lake to buy several dozen minnows and sometimes leeches. When we arrived at the lake, we put our car top aluminum boat in the water, attached the small outboard motor, threw our gear in the boat and took off. When we first starting fishing for walleyes, we used reels filled with twelve- or fourteen- pound test attached to stiff metal rods. On the end of the line was a lead headed jig most frequently colored orange, chartreuse or red with the hapless minnow or leech attached to it. We then proceeded out to likely spots and began trolling—as slowly as possible—bouncing the jig off the rocks on the bottom where the walleyes feed. When we felt a tug on our line, we waited several seconds for the walleye to eat the bait before we reared back and set the hook. The battle would last a few minutes before the fish was brought to net. As soon as that first walleye struck, we would toss a marker into the lake—a dumbbell shaped floating object with a stout line attached to it and a heavy weight on the end of the line. This marked the spot where the walleye had been hooked. We would then do circle eights around that marker (sometimes to no avail) hoping that we found a school of fish. If the walleyes were not hitting our baits while trolling, we would often stop at a likely hole and toss out our line and bobber fish. This can also be a very effective way to catch walleyes. In fact, the "stop and pop" method of bobber fishing is one that is preferred by fishing guides on big lakes such as Laker Saganaga where trophy walleyes frequently are brought to boat weighing ten pounds or more. As the years passed, we replaced the heavy fishing tackle with lighter spinning rods and reels loaded with eight-pound test and smaller jigs. But the method of fishing remained the same.

Walleyes are good but not spectacular fighters. The average walleye we were catching in the early days weighed maybe two pounds with the occasional lunker weighing six pounds or more. Our goal was to catch the limit of wallies, which I believe in those days, was six fish per person. With normally two fishermen in each boat, that was twelve total fish. Most days we caught our limit. In fact, my brother became so skilled at catching walleyes that he became known on the north shore as "Walleye Joe." In a period of over forty years, he brought to net thousands of them.

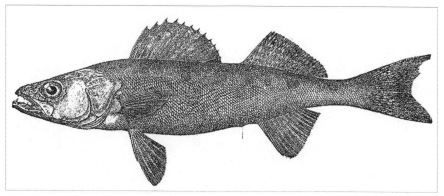

Walleyed pike. HUGH MCCORMICK SMITH, CIRCA 1907, UNIVERSITY OF WASHINGTON.

Our Walleye Lakes

The walleye lakes we fished in the Superior National Forest in the late 1960s, 1970s and beyond are almost too numerous to mention. A handful that stand out in my memory are Crescent, Silver Island, Rice, Kelly, Lichen, Timber, Freer, Parent and Axe. None of these lakes are huge, so they could be readily fished with a twelve-foot aluminum boat or a big canoe powered by a small outboard motor. The lakes basically fell into two different categories. There were a small number that were accessed relatively easily. They had a passable road into the lake and a landing of sorts. Crescent and Silver Island fall into this category. The others were son-of-a guns to get to.

Crescent was the very first walleye lake I fished on my initial trip to Tofte. It was late in the day, so did not take a boat out but fished instead from shore. I was awestruck by its beauty. Crescent Lake comprises 755 acres and has a maximum depth of 28 feet. It is located off the Sawbill Trail about 23 miles from Tofte. If you have never been to the Superior National Forest and the Boundary Waters Canoe Area, you must go. These lakes are spectacular in their beauty. The water is generally gin clear, huge dark boulders ring the shore and islands abound. Magnificent forests surround the lakes. I took one look at Crescent Lake and thought "My God, I can throw my line in here anywhere and I am sure to be rewarded with a big fish." Of course, we caught nothing. What did happen is that I was eaten alive by mosquitoes and black flies. (More about that later.) In spite

When fishing proved agonizingly slow on Crescent Lake, my brother would resort to bobber fishing in about fifteen feet of water at the rock pile." That's me snoozing in the front of the boat, while Joe is in the back waiting for all hell to break loose. DRAWING BY "WALLEYE JOE" ZUCKER, TOFTE JOURNAL, NOLAN/ECKMAN GALLERY (1994).

of my initial bad experience, Crescent was to become one of our favorite "go to" lakes that my brother and I fished for years to come—often joined by friends of my brother, my wife and my late father-in-law, Dr. Herbert Gornstein. Over the years, we caught hundreds of good-sized walleyes at Crescent. Although I was not along on the fishing trip that day, my brother once caught an eleven-pound walleye in Crescent. Today, Crescent has a campground and is heavily fished compared to back in the 1960s and 1970s, but the Minnesota DNR reports that it maintains a healthy walleye population along with northern pike, hybrid muskies and smallmouth bass.

Silver Island was the other easy access lake that we often fished. Dotted with many islands, this lake was—and still is—a walleye factory. But the wallies tend to be on the small side, averaging perhaps at little over one pound. It's a great lake to try when you need fish for the table or have been getting skunked at other lakes in the area. If you were taking a youngster on his or her first walleye expedition, I would recommend Silver Island because you are almost certain to catch a few. In the early years, we often camped on one of the lake's islands. This made sense because the islands were relatively free from biting insects, you could jump right in the lake off of the island for a refreshing dip and fish hot spots that were close at hand. Both sets of Zuckers had cats that we took camping. Joe and Susan's cat was an enormous orange tabby, Archie, who had a bad attitude; our cat, Budge, was a beautiful big grey and white feline. Both cats enjoyed camping, but they did not always enjoy each other's company on an island. I remember lots of hissing and snarling but they never got into a big fight.

Silver Island, in fact, saved the bacon for me on the first fishing trip my father in law made with me to the north Shore. Herbert loved fishing. Back in the 1950s, he fished Big Sandy (a huge lake about 136 miles north of Minneapolis) many times for walleyes and northerns. I remember him telling me a story about the day that he and his neighbor, Ed, caught so many northerns on Big Sandy that they had to keep rushing the latest limit them up to the lodge for the Indian guides to clean. Dad understandably wanted to return to Big Sandy, the scene of his great fishing success a decade or so earlier. I was adamant that we should fish the lakes of the North Shore. In the end, I won out. We tied my twelve-foot Montgomery Ward SeaKing aluminum boat on the roof of my 1972 Chevrolet station wagon, tossed his 1957 five-and-a-half horsepower Johnson outboard in the back of the wagon along with our fishing gear and struck out for Tofte. I was under heavy pressure to produce.

Fishing guide Charles decided the first day to take Herbert to Toohey Lake where I had had some success in the past. We trolled around Toohey for hours and did not get a single bite. Boy, did I hear it from my father-in-law. "I knew we should have gone to Big Sandy," he must have said a dozen times as I drove despondently back to our motel in Tofte. In my defense, the Minnesota DNR today describes Toohey as a veritable walleye factory, but also cautions that the walleyes can be difficult to catch in mid-summer because of the abundant number of fry perch in the lake. Perhaps that is the reason we struck out. The next day we fished Silver Island. Why I did not fish Silver Island the first day I do not remember, but I believe it because at the time after you turned off the highway to get to the lake the road was darned rough. In any case, we made it. Whew! The walleyes were biting like crazy. We caught dozens of fish and dad was a happy camper. It was the first of many successful fishing adventures on the north shore that I would share with him.

Camping on one of Silver Island's numerous lakes was wonderful for many reasons. We usually chose to camp on island # 9. It was a few miles down the lake, had a nice campsite and you could refresh yourself by diving off a rocky ledge into twenty feet of clear, cold water. Most importantly, because it was about a quarter mile from shore, it was largely devoid of the incessantly biting insects that patrolled the inland forest. Camping on an island, however, has one big drawback; especially if you have only one watercraft. That is, if some of the party who are camping on the island leave with the boat for the day to fish another lake, the people remaining on the island are stranded there. And that is exactly what happened many years ago when my brother, Susan, Shaya and myself were camped on island # 9 with our two cats, Archie and Budge. For same reason, Joe and I decided to fish another lake: maybe the fish were not biting at Silver Island or maybe we just decided to pursue bigger fish somewhere else. In any case, after a long day fishing a lake (I do not remember which one), we returned to Joe's station wagon to discover that it would not start: the battery was dead. We were in a pickle. We were way back in the woods in a remote area where someone might not come along for hours or perhaps until the next day. And the ladies were on the island with any way of knowing what had happened to us or of getting back to shore. And by 7 pm, we were rapidly losing daylight. Finally, a truck came along. Fortunately, the driver had some jumper cables. The station wagon's engine roared to life. We sped down the backwoods road as fast as we could towards Silver Island, reached the lake just as nightfall was setting in, threw Joe's boat in the water, and arrived back at the island just as it was turning dark. Susan and Shaya were happy to see us but understandably upset that had had to worry for hours about what horrible fate might have befallen us. The moral of the story: if you are camped on an island with one watercraft, do not take that watercraft to a different body of water.

That, of course, was not the only bonehead thing that the Zucker brothers and our fishing companions did during our years fishing on the North Shore. On another occasion, Joe, my brother's friend, Jim, and I were returning from fishing remote on McFarland Lake, located twelve miles from the tiny town of Hoveland located on the shore of Lake Superior. On the way back to the highway at about 4 p.m., we decided for some crazy reason to do a little exploring. We turned off of the secondary gravel road that headed back to Hoveland and on to an old logging road, thinking that perhaps we might discover a lake or stream filled with fish along the way. What we found, instead, was disaster. About one mile in, we crossed a narrow bridge spanning a small creek. What we did not know was that spring rains had caused the ground under the bridge to be washed away. About halfway across the creek, the road collapsed, and the station wagon sunk into the creek. Although the water was only about a foot deep, there wasn't any way to extract the vehicle from the muddy water, no matter how hard we tried. Now what to do? We had a flashlight but no bear spray (I am not sure it had been invented yet). And to make matters worse, Jim was terrified of black bears due to previous encounters he had had with them in the Superior National Forest.

We hoofed it back to the secondary road. But now which way to go? McFarland Lake had a nice lodge on it at the time. If we made it back the lake, we could perhaps get help there. Or, we could hike back down the secondary road until we reached Hoveland. If we made it to Hoveland, we had a good chance of hitching a ride from someone driving along Highway 61 back towards Tofte where we were staying. The only problem was we had no idea of how far it was back to McFarland Lake or down the secondary road to Hoveland. Jim and I were convinced that we were closer to McFarland Lake than Hoveland. My brother was sure we were much closer to Hoveland than McFarland Lake. We could, in fact, see the mist rising over Lake Superior from our elevated position in the backwoods, though we could not actually see the lake itself. In the end, Jim and I won out. We headed back towards McFarland Lake. Several hours later, exhausted and hungry, we arrived at the lodge. The hosts graciously provided us with something to eat and rented us a room at a reduced rate for the night.

The next morning, the lodge called a tow truck in Hoveland. A few hours later, the driver and tow truck arrived at the lodge. He was an elderly man of Finnish descent who said only a few words as he pulled the station wagon out of the muck: "Dumb shit kids." It turned out that Highway 61 was only three miles from the secondary road that we had turned off of and nine miles from McFarland Lake. I still wince when my brother and I discuss this event. "I knew we were closer to the highway," he says. "You and Jim should have listened to me." The moral of the story: Do not go adventuring down unknown roads late in the afternoon.

Fortunately, my brother, my wife and I, and my brother's fishing friends, were all young and in relatively good shape when we bushwhacked our way into the more remote Walleye lakes. One of my favorites is Rice Lake. This lake, like many other walleye lakes we fished, is relatively small—only 222 acres—and shallow, maxing out at a depth of only ten feet. I don't know about the road into Rice today, but in the 1960s and 1970s, it would have been a stretch to call it a "road." It was more like a muddy rut and a treacherous one at that. And I was not driving a rugged four-wheel-drive vehicle into Rice but rather my two-wheel-drive Chevrolet station wagon. Amazingly, I managed to damage only an oil pan in the many trips I made into the lake. My early trips into Rice were sometimes made with Grandpa Krueger, often accompanied by one of his fishing buddies, my brother and myself. Later on, when I acquired my own car-topper, my wife and I made many solo trips to Rice. It had terrific walleye fishing. We hoped for a west wind (walleye fishing is always best in a stiff west wind). This would allow us to troll slowly down the north shore of the lake into the wind. Bang! A dandy two to three pound walleye would be on the line. And then another. Rarely did we fail to catch our limit of walleyes and usually we had the added bonus of bringing numerous northerns to the boat. The lake has a beautiful island where we would stop for a picnic shore lunch—often consisting of freshly caught walleyes.

My brother reminded me in a conversation I had with him about the day we tried our luck on Rice after a huge storm had swept through the area the night before. The wind had so fierce that large trees had blown down. I told Joe that it was foolish to go: In my expert opinion, we would not get a bite. But Joe knew Rice like the back of his hand. He was confident we would get our limit. The wind was still howling when we arrived at the lake and the waves were so high that we wondered if it were wise to put our boat in the water. We decided to risk the waves and off we went. Joe said, "Lets head towards the east side of the lake. I think that's where they are going to be." We raced over to a bay where the wind was blowing the water on to the shore at a furious rate. The wallies had schooled up there, perhaps feeding on bait fish. It's hard to say how many fish we caught that day because it was more than fifty years ago. He thinks it might have been close to one hundred. It might have been.

Kelly Lake was another walleye gem that we often fished during our early years on the north Shore. Kelly is also a small lake. Long and narrow, it measures 173 acres and has a maximum depth of ten feet. Unlike Rice Lake, though, you cannot reach Kelly by a motorized vehicle. In order to access Kelly Lake, we had to first drive to the Baker Lake campground where we would park our car, throw the boat in the water and take off across Baker Lake, a shallow and weedy body of water, until we reached the far shore about ten minutes later. Then we had to line our watercraft (a boat or a canoe that could accommodate a small gas motor) down a treacherous rock filled shallow river for about a mile, all the while with hordes of mosquitoes and black flies trying to suck the blood from our bodies. Finally, we would make it the next put in on Peterson Lake. From Peterson (not a bad walleye lake it its own right), it was about a fifteen-minute trip to Kelly. Since the two are connected by a narrow but navigable stretch of water, we mercifully did not have to portage again. My first trip to Kelly was a memorable one. My brother, his friend, Jim Olson, and I were in Jim's motorized canoe. Jim was having engine trouble with his tiny three horse outboard. I thought we might have to turn around and call it quits. But finally, Jim's motor quit sputtering and stalling. We started to fish. I was in the front of the canoe. Heading towards an island at the far end of the lake, I was sure that my jig had hung up on rocks since my line had stopped dead in the water. But I set the hook anyway.

It wasn't a rock I was hung up on but a four-pound walleye. I caught the first three that day—one after another. All were in the four-pound category.

I would make many more trips back to Kelly before it became part of the Boundary Waters Canoe Area in 1978. The rules and regulations promulgated by the establishment of the BWCA prohibited the use of motorized watercraft on the lakes and rivers within its boundaries. This put an end to fishing expeditions on many of our favorite walleye lakes. Friends of the boundary waters fought indefatigably for years to secure its protection from development. In fact, they are still fighting battles to protect it today. I like to think of myself of as a defender of the wilderness, but I would be less than honest if I did not admit that losing some of those lakes was a blow. Of course, we could have continued fishing them in motor-less watercraft but that was simply not our *modus operandi.*

Timber Lake took the cake when it came to the difficulty involved in getting to the body of water we planned to fish. The lake has a surface area of 278 acres and a maximum depth of twelve feet. The Minnesota DNR states that Timber Lake today "offers some good opportunities to catch eater size Walleye for those willing to put in the effort to get to the lake." The MDNR adds that there are "no good direct accesses to Timber Lake," though the MDNR points out that it can be reached by a sixty-five-rod portage from Frear Lake (another good walleye spot) or a thirty-eight-rod portage from Elbow Lake. "Put in the effort," indeed! Since we were not paddling canoes through the lakes, the only way to get to Timber was to bushwhack through the forest. So, we would get as close to Timber as we could on what passed for a road, park our vehicles, unload our outboard motor and fishing gear and then begin to the arduous trek to the lake along a rugged trail. My brother, who is about six feet three inches tall and a former star high school basketball player during his high school years in Chicago, generally carried the motor. As the younger brother, my job was to carry the fishing rods, minnow bucket, lunch, boat cushions and so on. Often, we had a third fisherman with us who helped with the task. Generally, it took a few trips to ferry everything to the lake's edge. You ask, where was the boat? The boat had been hauled the mile or so to the lake on the very first trip to Timber.

After that, it remained there, hidden in the wood, covered up by a bunch of branches. This was—and, I believe, still is—in violation of Minnesota law. Of course, the park rangers eventually found our craft and hauled it away. My brother and I later saw the boat in the ranger station waiting to be auctioned off to the highest bidder. Do I feel badly about violating the law? I would be dishonest if I were to say that I have been wracked with guilt over the years by my participation in this misconduct.

Right: Me with a nice walleye, northern Minnesota, June 2005. AUTHOR'S COLLECTION.

Below: Me with a nice northern pike, also northern Minnesota, 2005. AUTHOR'S COLLECTION.

The Minnesotans Love Affair with the Walleye

What is the attraction that the walleye has for Minnesotans? Probably the number one reason for the Minnesotans love affair with walleyes is that they are delicious to eat. Among fresh water fish, I would rank them number one in terms of taste, though the Lake Superior white fish runs a close second. Baked, broiled or pan fried, they make wonderful table fare. Second, they are easy to clean, unlike the northern pike with its slimy skin and y bones. Even when cleaned by an expert, northerns can be tricky to eat—I have heard more than one story about a person choking to death on a y bone. Third, the walleye is abundant throughout most of Minnesota. According to the Minnesota department of Natural Resources, walleyes currently occupy about 1,700 lakes in the state totaling 2 million acres and 100 warm-water streams totaling 3,000 miles.

Alas, the MDNR states the average size of the walleyes being caught today has dropped off from earlier times because of fishing pressure. In Lake Winnibigoshish, for example, MDNR states that fishing pressure increased more than 700 percent from 1939 to 1977 while walleye yields (in pounds per acre) increased 150 percent. Most dramatically, however, the average weight of walleye that were kept declined from 2.2 pounds in 1939 to 1.3 pounds in the 1950s to 1.1 pounds in the 1970s. If Winnibigoshish is any indication, the average angler is catching fewer and smaller walleye. I saw this decline personally in the last few trips I made to the north shore in the late 1980s and early 1990s. We were still catching walleyes, but they tended to be smaller. It's also true that as we got older, we could no longer make the arduous trips into the remote lakes that we had fished in our youth where the fishing pressure was low or practically non-existent. No doubt pollution has also taken its toll.

How much do Minnesotans love walleyes? People are amazed to learn that in Minnesota walleyes were used as legal tender during its territorial years. That's right. According to a territorial law passed when Minnesota was a remote outpost of American civilization, Minnesotans could trade walleyes for goods and services that they needed. Now it was not unusual for animal pelts such as beaver and mink to be used as currency on the frontier, but

Minnesota was the only place that I know of where you could buy a sack of flour by plopping a two-pound walleye on the counter. Today, of course, Minnesotans no longer carry the walleyes around with them, but walleye currency is still used as legal tender alongside the US dollar. Walleye bills come in various denominations such as the one-pound walleye bill, the ten-pound walleye bill and the hundred-pound walleye bill. Perch coins are used for change. Four perch coins are worth one walleye dollar. With a couple of one-pound walleye bills today, you can purchase about three dozen good-sized minnows before heading out to the lake.

Walleye reserve note.

Mosquitoes: The Unofficial State Bird of Minnesota

If you love paddling through gin clear pristine lakes and camping in magnificent forests with the loon calling at dusk, then by all means you must go to the Superior National Forest. My advice, though, is, just do not go in June if you can help it. June is a month best reserved for the fanatical fisherman willing to risk his or her sanity to try to catch a walleye, northern pike, bass or trout. For, if you go in June, you may find yourself on the verge of hysteria caused by the unofficial state bird of Minnesota—the mosquito. The fishing in some of the hundreds of lakes in the SNF may have dropped off over the last fifty years for various reasons, but the mosquito population remains as robust as ever.

Alas, in some years, the mosquitoes remain intolerable throughout the summer. An article written by Dr. Craig Bowron in the August 22, 2014, edition of the *Minnesota Post* tells you all you need to know. Dr. Bowron writes that despite friendly skies and a perfect weather, a family trip to the BWCA quickly became a reprise of *There Will Be Blood*. He expected mosquitoes on the portages and at dusk but was unprepared for the swarms that made life miserable throughout the day. All the typical pleasantries of a trip through the boundary waters, he writes, were interrupted "by packs of little welts-on—wings." This plague, he learned from a mosquito expert, was caused by an unusually large snowmelt. And mosquitoes are only half the story, for Minnesota is also home to the black fly. These monstrous little pests crawl all over your neck and any other exposed part of your body. Their bite leaves angry, itching red welts.

I was totally unprepared for this one-two punch on my first fishing expedition to the north Shore. Standing on the shore of Crescent Lake, I was the victim of so many mosquito and black fly bites that I suffered an allergic reaction. The next day, my ears swelled up—I looked like Dumbo. So, it was off to the medical clinic in Grand Marais where the doc prescribed a course of antihistamines for me to take over the next week. I had learned my lesson. After that experience, I didn't dab insect repellent on myself before striking out for a lake—I practically took a bath in it. One June the mosquito and black fly population reached historic numbers. It was totally crazy to be camping out in the woods. But there Shaya and I were—in our tent at the Baker Lake campground. One morning, we awakened to what we thought was the pitter-patter of rain. "Oh," we thought, "it's raining. Might not be able to go fishing today unless it lets up." But when we opened the fly to our tent, we were surprised to discover that the sky above was blue. It wasn't rain that was bouncing off our tent but mosquitoes and black flies. We were horrified. We saw the young couple in the campsite next to us packing up their gear in an absolute panic. I am not exaggerating to say that they looked like they were about to lose their minds. Twenty minutes later they were gone. We stayed. Can't remember, though whether we caught any walleyes that day. Years ago, Shaya and I took a wonderful sea kayaking trip on Prince William Sound, which I discuss later on. People who had been to Alaska warned us. "The mosquitoes" they said, "will eat you alive." Were the mosquitoes bad? Yes, but nearly as bad as in northeastern Minnesota.

In Pursuit of the Smallmouth Bass

Although I enjoyed fishing for the walleye enormously during my Minnesota years, my favorite target was the smallmouth bass. Why? For me I think it is a matter largely of aesthetics. As I mentioned earlier, walleye fishing is much like hunting: since they are school fish, you spend large amounts of time—sometimes hours—bouncing a jig off the bottom of the lake before you catch one. This can grow tedious, especially if you are merely a "crew" member in the boat while the "captain" running the motor is making the decisions about whether next to try trolling past this rock pile or that drop off. Pursuing the smallmouth bass is a different story. True, you are going to get skunked more days fishing for the smallmouth bass than the walleye, but it is a more active kind of fishing. And when you hook one, they put up a terrific fight. One of the eternal debates that go on among anglers is whether the smallmouth bass or the rainbow trout is the best fresh water fighting fish pound for pound. Both are incredibly strong, and they are given to acrobatics when on the line. For me, it's a toss-up.

Out best smallmouth bass fishing fifty years ago or so was in the Boundary Waters Canoe Area. Many of these lakes, unlike the ones we were fishing farther to the south for walleyes, are huge and deep. And the best smallmouth lakes required portaging. If you are not familiar with portaging, let me tell you it is not an activity for the faint hearted. It requires placing all of your camping equipment, food and fishing tackle in a large canoe and then striking out across the first lake. When you arrive at the second lake, you must unload everything from the canoe and transport it all—including the canoe itself—across the portage to the second lake. Canoe portages are measured in rods. One rod equals sixteen feet. I have often thought that it must have been some diabolical woodsman who made the decision to measure the length of a portage in rods in order to deceive the unsuspecting novice. So, for example, if a tourist were to inquire at the ranger station about how far the portage is from lake A to lake B, the Ranger might tell him, "Oh, it's about one hundred rods." Not wanting to demonstrate his or her ignorance of such matters or perhaps in a hurry to start the expedition, the person fails to inquire how long a rod is. Little does he or she know that one hundred rods is the equivalent of more than five football fields. I was a young man when we portaged into BWCA lakes and even then I found it taxing. I remember seeing middle-aged men staggering across portages with their canoes raised above their heads. They had a look of utter desperation on their faces, perhaps wondering if the next breath they took might be their last. Of course, equipment has improved dramatically since then. We were ferrying heavy aluminum canoes across the portages and carrying heavy Duluth packs. And the rest of our gear wasn't exactly ultra-light either. I distinctly remember toting ice chests from one lake to the next.

Our favorite smallmouth destination was Rose Lake. The starting point for a trip into Rose Lake—and to many of the BWCA lakes—is Grand Marais on the shore of Lake Superior. The historic Gunflint Trail runs out of Grand Marais, winding its way through the heart of the Superior National Forest at the edge of the Boundary Water Canoe Area for fifty-seven miles before it ends at Lake Saganaga. In the old days, the Gunflint Trail was a gravel road; today, of course, it is paved. I don't remember how we found out there were big smallmouth in Rose Lake and that the best fishing for them was down in the narrows or "rat tail." Undoubtedly, some kindly angler was willing to share the information with us. The jumping off point for our canoe trips to Rose Lake was West Bearskin Lake—about a thirty-mile drive from Grand Marais. We paddled across West Bearskin until we reached the portage for Duncan. We then paddled across Duncan Lake to the portage to Rose Lake. After several hours (longer if we stopped to fish Duncan for smallies), we reached the campsites at Rose Lake. If we were lucky, the magnificent campsite high up on a bluff overlooking the lake would be open. If not, there were other nice ones scattered around the lake. You may be thinking, "Didn't they have reservations?" This was a different world. Almost all camping that I remember doing as a young man was first come, first serve.

After setting up our campsite, we would excitedly make plans for the next day's fishing. Alas, one tremendous chore remained to be done. If you access the Internet to find out about paddling to Rose Lake, the outfitters will inform you that it's only about four and a half hours round-trip from West Bearskin to Rose. Easy, they say. This may be true if you are traveling light and simply walk over the portage from Duncan to Rose to admire the breathtaking view. But if you are planning to actually put your canoe in the water on Rose Lake, you must negotiate the dreaded Stairway Portage. Negotiating the Stairway portage involves carrying you canoe down 130 wooden steps or so before you reach the lake. And, you must obviously reverse the process in order to get the canoe back up to the campsite. After breakfast, we hauled our canoe or canoes down to the water, arriving at a beautiful bay with Rose Falls to our right. You could catch fish right there, but we were interested in bigger game. So, off we paddled towards the narrows—about a forty-five minute trip. The narrows resemble more a river than a lake. It's maybe one hundred yards wide with lots of downed trees in the water—perfect cover for the smallmouth bass.

We did not know what to expect on our first trip into Rose, but it did not take long to find out. We tossed yellow Mepps rooster tail spinners (now considered a vintage lure) as close to the logs as we dared. Bang! An enormous smallie came rushing out from under a log, smashed the lure and flew high out of the water. My brother caught one that day that weighed over five pounds and we brought to boat several more that were in the three to four pound range. But catching them was not so easy. More often than not, in the midst of an acrobatic leap, the bass would throw the lure. Sometimes it landed right back in the canoe. Fish are curious critters. Often, when we were playing a smallie, a half-dozen or so bass bigger than the one we had on the hook would follow along behind it. After several hours of fishing, it was time to head back to camp. We were able to leave our canoes at the bottom of the Stairway Portage until the day we had to leave. Our first trip into Rose was perhaps our most memorable, but there were others where the smallmouth bass fishing was superb. All of them, though, were not fun and games. My brother and I made one trip into

Rose where we caught only a few fish. We were doomed to failure by blue bird skies and high pressure. Worse still, the biting bugs were horrendous. I was to catch smallmouth bass on several different lakes in the Superior National Forest as a young man—including football sized ones on Duncan Lake—but Rose Lake remained my favorite. Today, the smallmouth bass is expanding its range in the area, so they are easier to find. Crescent Lake, for example, has a good population of bass, though mainly in the one to two pound category. Only problem is that they compete with the walleyes. So, as the bass fishing improves in a lake, the walleye fishing tends to drop off.

Smallmouth bass. ILLUSTRATION FROM NEW YORK STATE COMMISSIONERS OF FISHERIES, GAME AND FORESTS, CIRCA 1896, UNIVERSITY OF WASHINGTON.

The Black Bears of the Superior National Forest

Years ago, my wife were staying in a pleasant RV campground in Buffalo, Wyoming. It had a nice swimming pool and, so, towards evening we decided to take a dip. People were conversing around the pool. A Danish man who was visiting the West with his family had just come from Yellowstone where he had encountered a black bear. He was very excited about this because, according to the literature that he had read, only "forty-five percent of the people who visited Yellowstone saw a bear." We were very happy for him but could not help smiling at each other. During our Minnesota fishing trips, it would have been quite unusual to see only one bear. Normally, we saw dozens. The black bear is not as dangerous as the ferocious and unpredictable grizzly bear that roams northwestern Montana. But it is still a bear and it can be dangerous. The thing is that modern methods of managing the bear population were unknown when we were camping in Minnesota in the 1960s and 1970s. Take garbage dumps, for example: No efforts were made to keep the bears out of them. In fact, they were a tourist attraction. Driving over to the local garbage dump at dusk to view the local black bear population sorting through the refuge for something tasty to eat was one of our favorite pastimes. And as bear attractants, the campgrounds were second only to the garbage dumps.

One year, Shaya, Susan, and I made an early August fishing trip into Rose Lake. My brother had just returned from another fishing adventure and was too tired to join us. But Joe reminds me that he did warn us about the bears. "Not a good time to go into Rose Lake," he cautioned. "It's late in the season and the bears are going to be active, looking for food before they hibernate." Of course, that did not stop us. And it's a good thing, too, from a fishing perspective that we went: the smallies were biting. We were down in the narrows one day on that trip catching bass, when I looked to the north towards Canada. My mouth fell open. A gigantic storm was rising over the hills. It looked like something of biblical proportions.

"My God, look at that" I said to Susan and Shaya.

"We better leave in a hurry," Susan cautioned. "We don't have much time before that storm hits." We put on our rain gear and began paddling furiously back to towards the Stairway Portage. As we pulled into Rose Bay, we were hit by a torrent of wind and rain. We made it to shore, pulled the canoes up on to the landing and headed up the stairs to our camp.

When we reached camp, we were surprised to see a young man sitting in front of our Eureka tent. This was alarming because people just do not normally just sit in someone else's campsite. But he immediately put us at ease. "I know this seems strange." he said, "I just wanted to tell you that a bear came through your camp while you were out on the lake." Okay, you are thinking that we should have hung our provisions up in the tree at least ten feet above ground. But we had not. The young man, in fact, had arrived at our campsite just in time to see the bear snatching my wife's

Duluth pack from under a picnic bench. The bear had carried the pack up the trail where it tore into it, tasting everything, including our toothpaste and my wife's watercolors. Short work was made of our left over fish. Probably our big mistake was cooking smallmouth over an open fire for dinner the night before. The bear undoubtedly had been attracted by the smell of the fish and had waited for us to leave camp before making its raid. With the storm raging, we invited the young man into the tent with us. Turned out he was an art student at the school in Minneapolis where my brother had taught (small world) for several years.

As we huddled in the tent, Shaya said, "The bear is back." Now there's a long history in our family of me poo-pooing my wife when she hears something outside the tent.

"That's crazy," I have a habit of telling her, "You are imaging things." Of course, she is almost always right. In this case, when the storm finally was over several hours later and we had emerged from our tent, her pack was gone from under the picnic table. The bear had returned and carried it up the trail again! With little food left and the bear in the vicinity, we had no choice but to high tail it out of there the next day.

The bear at Rose Lake was a single marauder but in the larger Superior National Forest campsites, big numbers of bears roamed about freely. One year, my brother, his friend Al and I were camped on Ninemile Lake located approximately sixteen miles northeast of the tiny town of Finland. The USDA Forest Service maintains a campground on the northeast side of the lake. This lake is picture-postcard beautiful. In fact, it is so beautiful that it reminds one of the Minnesota lakes featured in the Hamms Beer commercials of years past. "From the land of sky blue waters," was the refrain, as the TV showed a cartoon bear looking out of over a pristine lake. Joe and I were in one tent and Al was in another at our campsite. My brother likes to keep things organized, so he had a pup tent behind our tent filled with cooking provisions—no meat or anything like that—but things like flour, salt and pepper, and our cooking utensils. Every night a bear would show up after dark and begin rummaging through the pup tent, looking for something to eat. Joe would get out of his sleeping bag, crawl out of the tent and chase the bear away. I remember him running down the trail behind our campsite, hollering at the bear.

We thought hanging a lantern between our two tents might deter the bear but to no avail. The bear came anyway. We knew when it had arrived because the light hanging between our tents would suddenly be blotted out as the bear crept by. Ninemile Lake has about twenty campsites and it was close to full when we arrived. After about one week, Al, Joe and I noticed that the campers were beginning to thin out. The marauding bears were taking a toll. One evening, a young couple showed up at the campsite next to us. They were on their honeymoon. The bride said to her new husband after they had pitched their tent, "This is so beautiful. It looks like it is right out of a Hamms beer commercial." Hamms beer back in the day featured a cartoon bear looking out over a pristine Minnesota lake. I did not say anything to her but thought to myself, "She does not know how prophetic that is." The newlyweds had a cooler that they foolishly left outside. A bear, of course, visited their campsite that night, tossed the cooler around and tore things up. I saw them in the morning, a look of panic in their eyes, frantically throwing their camping gear in the car. In less than an hour, they were gone.

A few days later, the entire campground was deserted except for us. That's when the Park Ranger showed up. After the usual pleasantries had been exchanged—"how's the fishing been" and that sort of thing—he got down to business. "You boys will have to leave," he announced. We were dumbstruck. "But, why?" we asked. His reply was, "There's a fourteen day limit on camping in this campground and you have been here fourteen days." This was the height of absurdity. "But we are the only ones still here," we protested simultaneously. "Everyone else has left because they are terrified of the bears. Why don't you do something about the bears?" After some further discussion, we were allowed to stay for a few more days and the Ranger agreed to do doing something about the bear infestation. The next day a Forest Service truck showed up with a single bear trap in the back. The Ranger placed the trap down at the end of the campground. The next morning after breakfast, we walked down the trail to see if a bear had been trapped. Sure enough. There was a smallish black bear looking out forlornly from its new prison. We felt sorry for the animal. In my memory, we let the bear out of the trap. But that is not what happened. Al remembers that we had planned to open the trap door to let the bear escape but decided against it. The bear was left to its fate

Black bear. DIEGO DELSO, WIKIMEDIA COMMONS.

Fishing with My Father-in-Law: The Northerns of Moore Lake

On one of the trips that Herbert made with me to the North Shore, we both reached the point where we needed to take a break from fishing for walleyes. He loved to fish for northern pike and so did I. But where to go? Some of the lakes in the area contained monster northerns, but those lakes were all hard to get to. I wanted to find a lake where the action for northerns was likely to be fast and furious. On our trips to walleye lakes, we frequently passed Moore Lake. It had the reputation of being filled with the toothy monsters and it was an easy haul to get my twelve-foot Montgomery SeaKing twelve-foot aluminum boat down to the water. The Minnesota DNR describes Moore Lake as about sixty-one acres in size with a maximum depth of eight feet. It is very weedy—perfect cover for old *Esox lucius.*

After about a forty-five minute drive we arrived at Moore. We tossed the boat in the water and took off. I attached a big spoon to my heavy-duty leader and began casting as we trolled slowly down the middle of the lake. It did not take long before I had a strike. A dandy four-pound northern was on the line. After a brief battle, I netted the fish. Moore Lake was as advertised. As I was netting my fourth or fifth northern, I noticed that dad had not caught a single fish. After I had landed the northern, I looked up to the prow of the boat where dad was seated. He had his tackle box on his lap—he was organizing his fishing gear! Now, maybe it was because he was a doctor that all his tackle had to be perfectly in order. For example, he still had the boxes for fishing reels that he had purchased decades before. After a fishing trip was over, he would place his reels back in their boxes. Such meticulous care for one's fishing gear is admirable, but the fact is that you can't catch a fish if your line is not in the water. I remember shouting, "For God's sake, Dad, put your tackle box down and start fishing!" He took my advice and began casting. Soon he was catching northerns, too. We each caught our limit and then some, though none of Moore Lake's northerns weighed more than four pounds. It was a fun day. One thing about my father-in-law: Since he practiced general surgery, he had no problem cleaning northern pike. And he enjoyed eating them too. Northern are not bad eating if you don't mind worrying about getting a bone stuck in your throat. Some people pickle them, which takes care of the bone problem. Funny thing. When I was fishing with Dad back in the day, he looked really old to me. Now when I look at photographs of him from that era, he looks quite young. I wonder how that could be?

Fishing the Poplar River: The Brook Trout of the North Shore

I am not certain what the year was the first time I fished the Poplar River for brook trout with my brother. It might have been 1966 or 1967. One thing is for certain: It was a long time ago. Although we fished many brook trout streams together over the years on the North shore of Minnesota, the Poplar was the one we fished the most. And with good reason. I believe that back then the Poplar was one of the best brook trout streams in America.

Brook trout. ILLUSTRATION FROM NEW YORK STATE COMMISSIONERS OF
FISHERIES, GAME AND FORESTS, CIRCA 1896, UNIVERSITY OF WASHINGTONS.

It probably still is. The average brook trout we caught were in the eight to ten inch range, but we often brought to net brookies in the fourteen to sixteen inch range. The Poplar River stretches 21.7 miles from its source in Gust Lake to its mouth in Lutsen, where it empties into Lake Superior. Its major tributaries are Mistletoe Creek, the Tait River, Caribou Creek, and Barker Creek. It drains an area of 114 square miles.

Brook trout are native to headwaters and small streams of northeastern and southeastern Minnesota but have been introduced to many parts of the state. Their preferred habitat includes headwater spring ponds and small spring-fed streams that have cool, clear waters with sand and gravel bottoms and moderate amounts of vegetation. They also congregate behind beaver dams.

What made the brook trout fishing on the Polar so good? First, the Poplar was loaded with brookies. Thousands of them. Second, the Minnesotan's fascination with pursuing the Walleye meant that fewer fisherpersons were interested in fishing for trout, so the Poplar was lightly fished—even by the standards back then. Seeing another trout fisherperson on the Poplar was a rarity. Third, fishing the Poplar was not for the timid angler. No, sir. It was treacherous work for the river is narrow, rocky and the current is frequently strong. And since we did not have much money back then, our equipment was, to say the least, rudimentary. We fished in tennis shoes, wore blue jeans and a shirt of some kind. We most definitely did not have wading boots, waders or even a real wading staff. We slung a trout creel over our shoulder, which also contained our bait—nightcrawlers. (Sorry, trout-fishing purists, but I would not pick up a fly rod until many years later.) We carried spinning rods loaded with four-pound test and a net. Somewhere along the way we would pick up a stout stick and use it for a staff.

Old logging roads criss-cross the Poplar and depending on water conditions, we would head out to one section or another early in the morning. Once we parked our vehicle, we would hike up stream for a mile or two through the woods. Sometimes, we had to get in the water and wade upstream because the tangled brush made it impossible to make headway on shore. Once we were to our appointed spot, we would start fishing downstream. This involved putting a big chunk of nightcrawler into the current and letting it bounce off of rocks, until a trout grabbed it—which frequently did not take long. Big pools held lunkers. In the fast current, catching the brookies was a challenge, especially if you tied into a big one. The sixteen inchers frequently broke the line or threw the hook. This was catch and eat fishing. My brother, who had become a master at fishing the Poplar, usually caught at least two trout for every one that I caught. By the end of the day, we usually had our limit and would later enjoy a wonderful dinner of freshly caught trout back at our cabin or campsite. But I would not be telling the truth if I did not admit that we did get skunked. Bluebird days were to be avoided like the plague and the fishing could be poor if the water level were too high or too low.

Turnabout is fair play when it comes to fishing. Just as the walleye fishing could be unpredictable so could the brook trout fishing. Earlier in this story, you may remember that I told my brother we would not get a bite on Rice Lake one day because of the wild storm that had blown through the night before—and we wound up catching dozens of fish. Well, many years ago, Shaya, Joe and I were on a fishing trip on the North Shore. We had been getting our limit of walleyes, but Shaya and I wanted to take a break from trolling. We were eager to go brook trout fishing. One morning, the three of us had our usual discussion of where we were going to try our luck that day. These meetings were akin to generals deciding where they were going to deploy their troops in battle. Should we go for walleyes; and, if so, what lake should we try? How about Silver Island? That had lake been fishing really well lately, but the fish had been on the smallish side. Then there were discussions of the various merits of other lakes—Crescent, Rice and so on. This morning my wife and I were in agreement: We wanted to fish for trout. Joe said, "This is terrible day to go brook trout fishing. The weather forecast says there's going to thunderstorms. One clash of thunder will put the brookies down. We won't catch a fish." The weather, indeed, did look ominous. Large, threatening clouds gathered above our cabin. But we were adamant: It was brook trout fishing or bust. So, off we went in Joe's beater jeep.

The stretch of the Poplar we selected to fish was one of the most remote. It involved a two-mile hike around a mountain before we would begin fishing. Then, once we put our line in the water, it would be more than a mile downstream until we reached the take-out point where our vehicle was parked. Alas, the weather did not improve on the long drive out to the Poplar. If anything, it looked even worse. But we decided to hike into the river anyway. By the time we arrived at the spot where we would begin fishing, thunder was booming, and it had begun to rain. I know, we were crazy. The thought crossed our minds that we could be hit by lightning, but we were young and perhaps a tad foolish.

It did not take long to discover that the trout were biting—like crazy. It turned out to be one of the best fishing days that the three of us would enjoy together on the Poplar. It seemed almost magical catching trout in a thunderstorm. Physically, fishing the Poplar that day was even more brutal than usual. Without wading boots, waders and an actual wading staff, I cannot tell you how many times I fell down in the river, getting soaked in the icy cold water. Towards the end, I remember nearly breaking into tears (okay, I did beak in to tears but only for a moment) from the punishment the Poplar had dished out. Somewhere along the way, I managed to get ahead of Joe and Shaya who were worried because they did not know where I was. When they finally caught up with me, I got a good scolding. (Shaya could tell you that wondering off while trout fishing is a bad habit of mine.) Although this day on the Poplar happened more than forty years ago, the big one that got away still stands out in my mind. We were no more than fifteen minutes from the take out point when a gigantic brook trout nailed my nightcrawler. The battle was on. I had the trout right in front of me—eyeball to eyeball—when it threw the hook. I was heartbroken. But still what a wonderful memory to relive after all these years. Finally, we were at the take-out point and slogged wearily but happily back to the jeep for the long ride back to the cabin.

Brother Joe's Amazing Fishing Journals

Remarkably, my brother documented each day of his fishing expeditions on the North Shore for more than forty years. After returning to the cabin and cleaning his catch, he sat down at the kitchen table with pen in hand to carefully report on the action. What species of fish was he pursuing? What lake had he gone to? What were the fishing biting on? How big were they? What were the weather conditions like? Who were his fishing partners? And, most importantly, how had he faired? He also kept a running tab on how many of each species of fish that he had brought to net. Amazingly, Joe still has hundreds of fishing reports spanning several decades in his possession. My sister-in-law, Britta, was kind enough to sift through them, looking for ones in which I was included. Bingo! She found a span of nine days of his journal from June 9 through June 18, 2005, on what was quite possibly was my last trip to the North Shore. On June 10, we made our first outing together and I received the honor of making the entry in the journal for that day. I reported that:

> "Brother Joe and I went to the Popular River behind the Lutsen ski area. The weather started out nice, but it soon clouded up. My ancient Penn Reel broke almost immediately, so we took turns fishing. The fishing was not fast and furious, but we caught trout at a steady rate. Many were mediocre. Brother Joe lost a giant brook trout—the biggest he had ever seen. We waded down to the dead water where I was rewarded

with a dandy 14 (inch) trout. It started pouring. Soon there was thunder and lightning. So, we quit. The hike back through the alder trees proved to be great fun.

4.5 trips/51 trout

On the following day, Joe reported that:

"Charles and I spent a good day pounding wallies in Silver Island. We must have caught 80 Wallies keeping a nice limit of 11-4 to 11-2 pounders. The Kenny's island area was the best. The wind was N.E., E, SE. and of course it rained. We also saw a bear the way out. We used an entire pail of minnows.
Score: Wallie, 12 trips, 85 fish."

My trip also included an overnight guided fishing expedition for big walleyes on Big Saganaga Lake bordering Canada. The Gunflint Lodge website declares that the lake "is considered one of the finest walleye lakes in Minnesota, with hogs caught almost every day (twenty-eight or longer)." Although our guide was excellent, the fishing was slow—very slow. Joe reported on June 13 that we had fished for "9 hrs. with Lindy Rigs and leeches and got 3 keeper wallies had two or 3 misses, a couple of Bass, and one little norty." In his last five trips to Sag, he concluded that he had caught only "10 fish: not a good record." The weather on our trip didn't help. It was "hot variable to NO wind, poor conditions prevailed." To be honest, I was never enthusiastic about fishing Saganaga. I simply do not have enough patience to fish the endless hours it can take to hook a big one on Big Sag. But, make no mistake about it—they are there. Joe would catch several monsters in Big Sag over the years, some of them exceeding ten pounds.

We had a few more terrific days fishing during that trip. On June 15, we made the trek to Crescent Lake to try our luck fishing for smallies. The smallies were not biting all that well, but not to worry. Joe reported that evening that:

"we found dozens of nice walleyes close in to the shore in the far east bay. We must have caught 70 wallies, encountered a good sized muskies and hooked about 15 smallies. The wind was N. NE, NW and gusty! Score: Wallies 15 trips, 106 fish."

On June 16, we returned to the Popular, where I reported in the evening that:

> "The trout were voracious.... We must have caught one hundred on nightcrawlers on the Upper Reaches of the Popular. The weather was beautiful—a blue sky and warm.
>
> Not your classic trout day, but the trout did not know this. We kept about 18. The largest was about 14 inches."

All too soon it was time to head back to Duluth for the long flight home, but I took with me memories of yet another wonderful fishing trip on the North Shore.

CHAPTER IV

Transitioning from Northern Minnesota to the West

Moving to Austin

1988 was a momentous year for the Zucker family, for that was the year we moved from Champaign-Urbana, Illinois, to Austin, Texas. To tell you the truth, I never expected to wind up living in the Lone Star State—especially for more than thirty years. But you never know what fate has in store for you. Late in 1987, a colleague called to tell me that a job was opening up in Austin that he thought I should apply for as the director of a brand new faculty association. I admit that I had a classic Yankee response to the idea of moving to Texas. I informed my colleague that he was out of his mind—I would never move to Texas. But my colleague added, "Charles, Austin has a great quality of life. You should check it out." What did I have to lose? I flew down to Austin to interview for the job a few weeks later.

A month or so after that my wife made the trip with me to look Austin over. It was in early March. Everything was green and flowers were blooming. The temperature was in the seventies. The city was drop-dead beautiful. In case you have never been to Austin, it sits on the edge of the Texas Hill Country. The Hill Country does not fit the stereotypical view of Texas as a state composed of endless flat parched ranch land. In fact, gin clear spring fed rivers flowing over limestone and lined with bald Cyprus trees run through it: Among my favorites are the Frio, the Guadalupe, the Blanco and the San Marcos. And gorgeous Barton Creek flows right through the city of Austin, ending up at spring fed Barton Springs pool where the water temperature remains sixty-eight degrees year round. We were impressed. Even more so when on the flight home we landed in a horrible blizzard in St. Louis. It took me thirty minutes to scrape the ice off the windshield of our car. Shaya and I looked at each other and the decision to relocate in Austin was made right then and there. "Let's have a garage sale," she said, "and sell the snow shovels."

The move to Austin would precipitate a major change in my fishing world. Tofte, Minnesota, was now more than a 1,400-mile drive from my home and not an easy destination to reach by airplane. My gaze would in the future be towards the West.

Fly Fishing the Texas Hill Country: Barton Creek and Beyond

When did I first pick a fly rod and go fishing? I wish I could remember, but I know it was sometime after we moved to Austin. Austin, Texas, in 1988 might seem like an improbable place to take up fly fishing, except for one thing: It had a legendary fly shop, the Austin Angler. When the proprietor, Larry Sunderland, first opened in 1980, people thought he was crazy. Texas, after all, is a state dedicated to the pursuit of the largemouth bass. This generally means racing in your $15,000 bass boat across a huge reservoir until you reach your destination where you begin tossing a large spinner bait or plastic worm in the murky depths. But the Austin Angler would stay in business on South Congress Avenue for twenty-four years until Larry was forced to call it quits because he could no longer compete with the Internet. Several years after I had taken up fly fishing, I took my reel into the Austin Angler to get it cleaned. Pieces of leader material were tangled inside the fly line. The reel itself was encrusted with sand and grime. I was embarrassed. Larry was behind the counter. I remember apologizing to him for bringing such a sorry looking mess into the shop. He took one look at it and said, "What, are you kidding? This is great. You have been out fishing a lot with this reel." He went to explain that he had lots of anglers bring their fly reels in for cleaning that had been used only a few times. I suddenly felt much better. I am sorry to say the Austin Angler was the kind of place that has largely disappeared from American life. It was not just a store where you went to buy some fly-fishing gear. It had a strong sense of community. People stood around and talked about fly fishing, swapping stories and adventures. Try doing that today when you are ordering your tippet material and leaders online from AvidMax.

But back to the story of how I first took up fly fishing. I needed some persuading. In the 1980s, the Texas Department of Parks and Wildlife began stocking trout in the Guadalupe River tail waters below Canyon Lake dam. And Trout Unlimited soon followed suit. Today, the Guadalupe trout fishery is a huge deal. Thousands of fisherpersons flock to it annually during the winter months to try their luck. Back in the late 1980s and early 1990s, it was not yet that popular. The Guadalupe below Canyon Lake is about an hour south of Austin. I began making trips to the river to try my luck for trout using my spinning gear. For bait, I would use a piece of corn, a worm or some of the trout attractant goop. One day, I was spin fishing on the Guadalupe. Standing downstream in the river about fifty yards from me were three fly fishers. They were immaculately outfitted in expensive fly-fishing gear from head to toe (well, I actually could not see their toes). They looked very intense as they made casts and retrieved their wet flies. I watched them for the better part of an hour. Nothing. Nada. Not a bite. "Hum," I thought to myself. "Why would anyone take up fly fishing? It seems like a total waste of time."

A few days later, I stopped by the Austin Angler. I do not remember the name of the woman who was behind the counter. But I do remember asking her a question. "Why," I said, "would anyone in their right mind take up fly fishing?" I then explained that I had witnessed three fly fishers standing in the Guadalupe in the same spot for an interminable amount of time without so much as getting a fish on the line.

"Let me ask you a question," she said to me. "What would you do if you were fishing in a spot in the river for fifteen or twenty minutes and you did not get a strike?"

I answered without hesitating. "I would move," I said.

"Exactly, those fishermen were posers. They looked like they knew what they were doing but they did not have a clue," she said.

"Oh," I said. That was all the convincing I needed.

Sometime shortly after that, I took my first fly-fishing lesson from Joe Robertson (one of the Hill Country's best fly fishers) in the alley next to the Austin Angler.

Sorry to say that my first fly-fishing outfit did not come from the Austin Angler. I was on a tight budget and, so, made a trip to a local big box store where I picked out an inexpensive rod, reel, and line. I also outfitted myself for the first time with inexpensive waders, vest and the rest of the necessary fly-fishing paraphernalia. To be honest, I do not remember where I first made a cast with a fly rod: it may have been in the Guadalupe. What I do remember, though, is attending a Christmas holiday party hosted by a neighbor in Lost Creek, a subdivision on the edge of the Texas Hill Country where we had purchased a home in 1990. Somehow, the conversation turned to fly fishing. My neighbor informed me that he had gone fishing on Barton Creek and had caught quite a few. He seemed almost apologetic about fishing in Barton Creek. I was surprised. "Fish in Barton Creek?" I asked. "That doesn't seem possible." Why I thought it was not possible now seems puzzling to me. But what did a Midwestern boy know about fishing Texas Hill Country streams?

I had to wait for the weather to warm up. A few months later when the trees had started to bud out, I took the five-minute drive from our house to the bridge that crosses over Barton Creek. I waded downstream from the bridge with high cliffs on my right and trees on my left. Barton Creek at this point is perhaps thirty feet wide. I tossed out a dry fly—what it was I do not recall. On the third or fourth cast, a fish came up from the depths and grabbed the fly. My mouth fell open. That day I caught an assortment of nice sized freshwater fish, including the beautiful Guadalupe bass, a native to the streams and rivers of the Texas Hill Country. This was the first of dozens and dozens of fishing trips I would make to Barton Creek over a period spanning more than two decades.

What I loved most about fishing Barton Creek was the intimacy: The fish were right in front of me. Typically, I would arrive at the creek in the morning around eight a.m. and fish until eleven or so. If it were early in the year and the water still chilly, I would don my chest waders. Later in the year, I would fish in water shorts. I fished with either my four-weight or five-weight fly rod depending on the conditions. Almost all the time, I was using some sort of surface bug—typically, a chartreuse popper or a buggy-looking fly. Sometimes, though, if I could not entice the fish to hit on the surface, I would use wet flies. Moving slowly down the stream, I constantly evaluated where to throw my fly. I learned quickly that the fish liked to hang close to the bank or behind rocks. My casts were no longer than fifteen or twenty feet. Cloudy warm days when it was threatening to rain were the best. Sunny days were tough. The whole stretch of water I fished was no more than a mile long.

Most of the fish I caught were what Southerners call "perch" but what those of us from the North call "panfish." There was an assortment of bluegills and sunfish—some of them quite large. But there were also bass. In addition, to the previously mentioned Guadalupe bass, Barton Creek also is home to smallmouth and largemouth bass. The biggest bass that I was to catch on Barton Creek easily weighed four pounds. I hooked it on a wet fly only a few feet from where I had started fishing. The creek, though, held much larger specimens than that one. On several occasions, I had monsters come out from the depths to try to eat a panfish I had on the line. Talk about an adrenaline rush!

The first year I fished Barton Creek was a bonanza. I caught dozens of bass and too many panfish to count. It was exciting fishing. The second year was also excellent but not as good as the first. And then it began to go slowly downhill. I still would have many, many wonderful days fishing the creek, though the days I returned home a happy fisherman become more and more infrequent. And some years were pretty much a total bust. This was, in fact, one of three experiences in my life fishing a body of water— or a region—where the first year would prove to the best. I sometimes wonder if this has something to do with the fishing gods. Do they entice you in only so they can disappoint you later? I wonder if you have had a similar experience.

Why did the fishing on Barton Creek decline? I hardly qualify as an expert on the subject of ichthyology. However, I believe several factors came into play. First, when fishing streams or rivers, water levels are extremely important. If the water is too high, the fishing stinks. If the water is too low, it is also bad. Northerners may find this hard to believe, but in August I could walk down stretches of Barton Creek without so much as getting a toe wet where I had caught fish a few months earlier. Bone dry. So, in some years, the water conditions were just not favorable. If we did not have enough rain in the fall and winter, the fishing was lousy. I do not have any charts and graphs to prove it, but I believe as time went on, we had more years when there just was not enough water in the creek to support a healthy population of fish. They second factor was the development of Austin itself. When we moved to Austin in 1988, it was still a relatively small city, home to UT-Austin and the state capitol. Sometime in the mid-1990s, that began to change. Austin began to grow at a phenomenal rate. This meant an enormous amount of urban sprawl. The pollution of Barton Creek became a serious issue as run off from rainstorms dumped chemicals of all kinds into the water. The Austin environmental community, led by the Save our Springs (SOS) organization, would force the city council to pass one of the strongest environmental laws in the nation. But the law could not stop the endless suburban developments for miles on both sides of the creek. The third factor, which was a direct consequence of the second factor, was the growing use of Barton Creek. It's a wonderful place and I am happy so many people are able to enjoy it. However, in my final years of fishing the creek, it became more and more crowded—not only with other fisherman but by people in general.

Two of my other favorite Hill Country Rivers to fish were the San Marcos and the Pedernales River. The San Marcos arises from the San Marcos Springs, the location of Aquarena Springs, in the city of San Marcos (the home of Texas State University). It flows for seventy-five miles before joining with the Guadalupe River. Aquarena Springs Lake itself is well worthy of a visit if you find yourself traveling up or down I-35. The water is crystal clear. In fact, so much so that glass bottom boats take school children and tourists out on the water. My wife and I were scuba divers and for many years served as volunteers at the Springs. Our job was to clean algae and other debris off of the bottom of the lake. When boats passed overhead, we would wave to the passengers. The Springs were a popular amusement attraction during the 1950s and 1960s when it was privately owned. A fake submarine with glass windows allowed guests to view "mermaids" swimming in the lake. Perhaps the biggest hit was Ralph, the diving pig, who had been trained to jump off a diving board. All that is gone now. Aquarena Springs today is a serious science and research center operated by Texas State.

My favorite place to fish the San Marcos was at Tom and Paula Goynes' San Marcos River Retreat, a beautiful campground located on the shores of the river. Tom founded the Texas Rivers Protection Association and for many years served as its president. This is a remarkable organization that for decades has fought heroic battles against those who would destroy the state's beautiful rivers. I was honored to serve on the board of the TRPA for many years. For an admission fee of a few dollars, I could park my car at Tom and Paula's campground, don my fly-fishing gear and begin wade fishing up and down a stretch of the river for a mile or so. My favorite time of year to fish the San Marcos was in the fall, which in central Texas meant October and early November. I would toss a big popper close to one bank or another and wait for a big bream to come up from the depths and grab it. If I were lucky, a nice sized bass might take my popper.

Secondary roads criss-cross the San Marcos, but it is not easy to find a place where you can park you vehicle. "No Parking" signs abound at bridges crossing the river. The same is true for the other Hill Country rivers such as the Blanco, the Frio, the Guadalupe, the Pedernales and the Llano. Texas, in fact, is not a state dedicated to public access to its rivers. The truth is it's downright hostile. Some of the biggest battles fought by the TRPA have been to gain public access to the state's rivers. In this regard, Texas is the polar opposite of Montana where public access to its rivers and lakes is zealously guarded by fishermen.

The nice thing about fishing the Pedernales is that it flows through a huge state park in the Texas Hill Country west of Austin. So, there's no problem with gaining access. I fished the Pedernales for many years, primarily for beautiful Guadalupe bass that averaged fourteen inches in length. According to Texas Parks and Wildlife, the Guadalupe bass is found only in the Lone Star State. Living in fast flowing water, it is found primarily in the rivers and streams of the Edwards plateau. I would park my vehicle at the "beach" parking lot and walk a few hundred yards or so down to the river. This section of the river is gorgeous. Flowing over limestone, it's in a canyon and the hillsides are adorned with trees, cacti, rock outcropping and wildflowers. I would walk up river for a half an hour or so before I began fishing a small wet fly for the bass. On a good day, I would catch a half-dozen or more in a few hours of fishing. Sophie, our Old English Sheep dog, often accompanied me on these expeditions. OESs are herding dogs, so they follow you wherever you go but they are not particularly fond of water. When I began wade fishing, Sophie would stand in a foot or two of water, looking absolutely pathetic. So, I would have to take time out from fishing to help her on to one of the big rocks in the river. Then she was a happy camper.

Onward to Idaho

The first year Shaya and I were married, we drove from Chicago up to Minnesota and then on to Canada accompanied by our camping cat, Budger. We traveled all the way from western Ontario to the shore of the Pacific Ocean in British Columbia and then back home again through the northern tier of the western United States. Shortly after our move to Austin, Southwest Airlines offered a terrific deal. You could fly anywhere that Southwest flew in the United States for one hundred dollars round-trip. We always remembered how beautiful northern Idaho was and wanted to return someday to explore it further. Once of the places that Southwest serviced was Boise (and still does). So, we bought tickets, send our boys off to visit their grandparents in Chicago, packed our camping gear and flew off.

Boise is actually located in a desert-y part of Idaho (in fact, a lot of the state is desert). So, we were a little surprised and disappointed when we arrived there for the first time to find ourselves in a hot, dry climate instead of surrounded by magnificent forests and mountains. But we picked up our rental vehicle, loaded up our gear and next morning began exploring. We drove north along Highway 55 towards McCall. About an hour outside of Boise, our spirits improved. We found ourselves traveling through the gorgeous scenery that we had remembered from our first visit to the state. We spent the first night camping on Cascade Lake. For Shaya, though, this was not be a pleasant vacation. A few days after our arrival, her eye began to hurt and then the pain became excruciating. We were able to make an appointment for her back in Boise with a specialist and so had to backtrack. It turned out she had a staph infection. The doc was terrific. He prescribed an antibiotic and the next day we were back on the road again.

Then things went from bad to worse. About a week into the vacation, we called the grandparents in Chicago to check on the boys and discovered that Herbert was in the hospital. He had taken too many aspirins and had begun bleeding internally. It was serious. That night we discussed what to do. Should Shaya fly to Chicago by herself or should we both go? After a lengthy discussion, we decided that Shaya should go alone. Somebody had to carry on with the fishing. So, we drove back to Boise again to drop Shaya off at the airport. (Herbert fortunately made a speedy recovery.) I still had at least ten days of vacation remaining—plenty of time to explore the vast wilderness of Idaho, which at that time I knew little about.

Fishing The Middle Fork of the Salmon River:
My First Big Idaho Adventure

While I was back in Boise I stopped in a fly-fishing shop. I had done some boning up on fishing in Idaho before we left on our vacation and I knew that the Middle Fork of the Salmon was reputed for its trout fishing. I remember saying to the man who waited on me that I wished that I could fish the Middle Fork but could not do so because I did not have a water-craft. He said to me, "Why would you need a boat?" "Well," I replied, "because it's a river in a remote area. How would I get there?" "You would drive," he answered. Of course! The inflatable rafts and kayaks had to get there somehow. There had to be put in and take out points. So, I hauled out my map of Idaho and he showed me exactly how to get there. I took State Highway 21 to Loman where I turned off onto the Bear Valley Road, which the USDA Forest Service describes as "rough and narrow." The Forest Service is right about that. The Middle Fork of the Salmon River is one of the most beautiful rivers in the United States. It runs through the huge Frank Church River of No Return Wilderness, which the Forest Service describes as an area of "steep, rugged mountains, deep canyons, and wild, white water rivers."

After a few more hours and some wrong turns, I arrived at the Dagger Falls campground on the busy Boundary Creek launch site. I made something to eat for dinner, pitched my tent and crawled into my sleeping bag for the night, and dozed off to sleep thinking about the adventure that awaited me in the morning. But before I turned in for the night I had met another fisherman who told me where to go. He said to me, "Hike down the trail that follows the river for about two miles. The trail will go away from the river. When it comes back to the river, that is where you want to fish. Put a big grasshopper imitation on your line." Before departing in the morning, I left a note on the windshield of my vehicle stating that I had gone fishing and if there were not any sign that I had returned in a day or two, the authorities should be notified. The directions were good. I arrived at the spot, rigged up fly rod and waded into the water. I did not bring my waders and boots with me because I did not want to carry all that gear on the hike. The water was freezing cold. I tied on the grasshopper and let it float downstream. I was shocked when a big cutthroat emerged from the deep and inhaled my fly. After a few minutes battle, I landed the prize. And then I caught another one. They were in the two to three pound category. The fishing was terrific that day, but I could only survive for about an hour in that icy water. My teeth were chattering, and I was starting to turn blue. So, I reeled in my fly line and hiked back to camp. The following year, Shaya and I would return to that exact spot. Of course, I had regaled her with the story of the huge cutthroats that I had caught. But what a difference a year can make. We fished for several hours and only had a few mediocre trout to show for our efforts. I hasten to add, though, that at this point we were both novice fly fishermen with very few tricks up our sleeves. We did not, for example, have a clue as to how to fish wet flies. An experienced angler might have done a lot better.

Henry's Fork of the Snake River: The River of Epicurean Trout

Another legendary trout fishery that I had researched before departing was the Henry's Fork of the Snake River. I still had plenty of time before I had to head back to Austin, so I packed up my gear and headed out on the six hour drive from the Middle Fork to the tiny hamlet of Island Park in extreme eastern Idaho, located and only a stone's throw from Yellowstone National Park. I found a campsite on the banks of the river and set up my tent. No reservation needed in those days. Fishing Henry's Fork was unlike any kind of trout fishing I had done up to that time. The river contains a veritable smorgasbord of aquatic insects. This means that the fish have

a lot to eat, so they grow fast and get very large. It also means that they can be extremely picky about what they eat. Thus, if you are fly fishing, you had better be pretty darned good at both presenting your fly and matching the hatch. Henry's Fork trout awake early in the morning to decide what they are going to eat that day. For example, for breakfast they might order Eggs en Cocotte (or *Oeufs en Cocotte* in French) served in red crockery. For lunch,

ROB BENIGNO, LAKESRIVERSSTREAMS.COM

it might be a *niçoise* salad and for dinner a *filet mignon* wrapped in bacon served medium rare. If anything is wrong with the order or it is not presented beautifully, it gets sent back to the kitchen. This is why hard-core fly fisherman from all over the world who plan to try their luck on the Henry's Fork practice their art for weeks before they arrive. It is challenging fly fishing, to say the least.

Some sections of the Henry's Fork of the Henry's Fork are open to dry fly fishing only, but others are open to spin casting. So, in the morning after my arrival, I tried my luck on a section where I could spin fish. Darned if the fish were not still biting! I caught several beautiful rainbows on French spinners in rapid water. But then it was time to try my luck fly fishing the Henry's Fork. One section of the Henry's Fork flows through a huge meadow that encompasses seven or eight miles of the river. Most of this part of the river is within the Harriman State Park. From 1902 to 1977, this land was the private retreat of the Harriman family whose ancestors had owned the Union Pacific Railroad. But in 1977, the entire parcel was deeded to the state of Idaho for free by Roland and W. Averell Harriman. It's a relatively easy section of the Henry's Fork to wade fish since much of it is shallow and the current is slow. I stopped by one of the many excellent fly-fishing shops located in Island Park to buy some flies and to get some tips on fishing this water. Then it was off to the state park.

I waded out to a likely looking section and began casting. Nothing. Then, about an hour after I arrived, a hatch erupted. Now, I have seen many hatches over the several decades that I have been fly fishing, but I have never witnessed another one like this. I was literally surrounded by hundreds—perhaps thousands—of trout surfacing to eat an insect that covered the surface of the water. I gathered up a few of the critters to see what they looked like and then frantically began looking through my fly box to see if I had anything that resembled the real thing. Ah, here was one that was close. A small grayish brown fly. I tied it on to my leader and began madly casting to the rising fish all around me. Darn. I could not get one to eat my fly. But then about ten minutes into the hatch, I caught one. Over the next half hour, I caught a couple more. The hatch ended as suddenly as it had started. Lunch was over. It's difficult to describe my emotions during this event. I was astonished and excited by the number of trout in the river, but I was also sorely disappointed to have only caught three. I reeled in my line and waded back to shore.

The Firehole River, Yellowstone National Park. MIKE CLINE, WIKIMEDIA COMMONS.

An impeccably outfitted fly fisherman with a wonderful British accent was standing on the bank when I arrived." "How did you do?" he asked.

I replied, "I am ready to check into the local insane asylum."

"Why is that?" he said.

"Because I was surrounded by thousands of trout," I whined, "and I only caught three." "Actually," he said, "You did not do that bad. When there's that much food in the water, it's hard to get a trout to focus on your fly. They have so much to choose from." We chatted for a few more minutes. He told me that he had been fly fishing on the Henry's Fork for three days and had yet to land a trout. I suddenly felt better.

How tough can it be to match the hatch on the Henry's Fork? Several years later, Shaya and I were wade-fishing a section of the river in Harriman State Park when a big hatch erupted. I tied on several different flies but had no luck. Then a guide and her client pulled up in a drift boat on the other side of the hatch. I thought to myself, "Okay, it's going to be interesting to see what this guide does to catch these fish." The client began casting. After about ten minutes, she changed flies. After about another ten minutes, she changed flies again. The fly changing went on for about an hour. But nary a trout was hooked. Finally, she pulled up her anchor and left.

Brown trout. ILLUSTRATION FROM NEW YORK STATE COMMISSIONERS OF FISHERIES, GAME AND FORESTS, CIRCA 1896, UNIVERSITY OF WASHINGTON.

Fishing the Firehole: Be Prepared!

Even though the Henry's Fork trout fishing was challenging, we returned many times over the years to the Island Park area. It was one of our favorite areas of Idaho and, as I mentioned, close to Yellowstone. In fact, many of the guides who fished the Henry's Fork also guided in the Park. One night as we were having dinner in a nice restaurant I overheard a guide at the next table mentioning to his companions that he had had a terrific day fishing the Firehole River inside Yellowstone. "Hum," I thought to myself, "the Firehole. I need to check that out." The Firehole is one of the most unique trout streams in the world. A major tributary of the Madison River, it flows through three of the largest and most active geyser basins in the world, including iconic thermal features. It was named by early trappers who saw steam arising out of the river. The heated water makes fishing the Firehole better in the early spring and late fall than in the summer months when the water simply gets too warm to hold trout. The river contains rainbows, brook trout, and brown trout.

The next day we drove to West Yellowstone and stopped in one of the many fly shops to learn more about fishing the Firehole. It was September, so grasshopper imitations were the fly of choice. Much of the Firehole is rapid water but we were informed that the best fishing was indeed in the geyser area where the river is more like a meandering mountain stream. So, we headed out to the river not knowing what to expect. After a few wrong turns, we found the section of the river we were looking for, parked our vehicle, donned our fly-fishing gear and walked across a broad meadow to the river. Along the way, we noticed grasshoppers jumping in front of us. Not just some grasshoppers but hundreds and hundreds of them. When we were at the riverbank, I saw that the hapless grasshoppers had no idea that there was a river in front of them. They jumped straight into the river where eager trout were rising to gobble them up.

Now, the Firehole is not noted for producing big trout. According to the numerous websites that discuss fishing the river, the average fish is maybe eight to ten inches, though it's not uncommon to catch some fifteen to eighteen inchers. So, I probably had a 4X leader tied on to my line. This is in the way of an excuse for what was about to happen. The brown trout that came out of the depths to inhale my grasshopper imitation was no eight to ten incher. If anything, it was more like eighteen inches and probably weighed in about four pounds. It snapped my leader as if it were made of the thinnest gossamer. And that was the story of the day. Shaya and I hooked at least a dozen of these behemoths but only managed to land a few. It was one of those amazing days of fishing where something totally unexpected happened. Any expert fly fisherman who read this account will, of course, think to him or herself, "Why didn't they change leaders and fish a 2X or maybe even a 1X?" Well, because, Charles did not have any heavier leaders or tippet material with him. You can pay a price for being a fly fisherman who is not prepared for any contingency. And that day we both did. Of course, the next morning we were back at the fly shop where I purchased much heavier leaders and tippet material. But you can guess what happened. The fishing that day was only fair. We had had our one shot at a very exceptional day of fishing on the Firehole.

Where those giant brown trout came from and where they went one can only guess.

Huge brown trout, though, were not the only thing that we were unprepared for on that memorable day on the Firehole. We had learned to carry bear spray with us on our outdoor adventures in the West. And we had it with us in the car that day. But, did we have it with us on the river? No. We had left our bear spray behind. "Why?" you might ask. Well, we were in a hurry to get down to the river and we did not think that bears would be wandering around out on the plains—they should be behaving like good bears and be in the forest. About two hours into the fishing, I heard some fly fishermen upstream from me hollering, "bear!" I looked up to see a bear crossing the river about one hundred yards from me but only a few yards from Shaya. Looked like a black bear to me from that distance. But it wasn't. It was a big old grizzly bear. Shaya later reported to me that she made eye contact with the bear who fortunately was not interested in her as a food item. It climbed out of the Firehole and meandered across the plains. The fishermen all exited the river, including us. We thought about leaving the river for good but when we noticed that all the other fishermen were gone, we took out our bear spray and went back to the river to continue fishing. I later thought that I should get a fake bear outfit to take with me on fly-fishing trips. If the river were crowded, I could don the bear outfit and scare the other fishermen away. The next day when we returned to fish the Firehole again, the park ranger at the West Yellowstone entrance cautioned us that a big grizzly had been spotted the day before at the river. "Really? We will be careful," we said, and were on our way.

Grizzly bear. GREGORY SLOBODIR SMITH, WIKIMEDIA COMMONS.

Fishing in a Ghost Town: The Dredge Ponds of Warren

On one of our vacations to Idaho, the fishing was dreadful. We were camping on the South Fork of the Salmon River and not catching a thing. Desperate to find a place where we might have better luck, we stopped into a ranger station to ask for advice. Fortunately, a ranger who was on duty knew something about fishing. "I have just the ticket for you." he said, "Try the dredge ponds up in Warren." We said, "The what, where?" He then explained to us that Warren, Idaho, was about a two-hour drive north of McCall mostly over gravel roads. Warren had been a mining town where gold was discovered in 1862. For the several decades, the gold was relatively easy pickins but then it began to play out. So, in 1931, a gold dredge was brought to the area to work the deep gravels. The dredge would prove to be so successful that three more were brought in by 1934. Dredging continued up until 1942 when it ended for good. Today, although it is considered a "ghost town," Warren boasts a summer time population of about fifty people. In recent decades, the dredge ponds now filled with water have been stocked with trout by the Idaho Department of Fish and Game.

So, off we went. After arriving in Warren, we were able to locate the roads to the ponds, but they looked sort of rough for a rental vehicle to negotiate. We did not want to get it stuck in a rut in the middle of nowhere; we turned around and headed back to town to eat lunch at the Winter Inn—Warren's combination café and saloon, to figure out what to do. I ordered the grilled cheese sandwich. (I forget after all these years what Shaya ordered.) We began talking to the bar tender/wait person about our dilemma. An elderly gentlemen sitting at the bar to my left turned to me and said, "I will take you fishing at the ponds tomorrow if you can tell me that you do not have expensive fly-fishing gear." To this day, I do not know why Barry asked me about our equipment. I never bothered to ask him what difference it made. I assured Barry that our fly-fishing gear was about as bottom tier as you get—fly rods and reels, etc., from the sporting goods section of a big box store.

"Fine," Barry said. "Meet me at my house tomorrow at 8 am." He told us where he lived, and we found a place up the road to pitch our tent for the night.

The next morning, we arrived at Barry's charming little house bright and early. We headed out in his truck for one of the ponds. The pond he chose to fish was loaded with brook trout. We had trouble catching them. Barry did not. I think the final total at the end of the day was Barry, thirty brook trout; Charles and Shaya, four. What was his secret? Although he was a far better fly fisherman than either of us, his expertise was only partially responsible for the big difference. The fly he was using also had much to do with his success. When we were finished fishing for the day, Barry showed us the fly: It was a renegade. The renegade, developed in the West in the 1920s, is an attractor fly that perhaps resembles a beetle to a hungry trout. Today, this fly has fallen out of fashion. Why, I don't know. I would bet you a dime to a dollar that should you walk into a couple dozen different fly shops in the West to ask what flies to use on a local river or lake, you would not walk out of one of them with a renegade. Yet, if I were to enter a trout-fishing contest in Montana (an unlikely event) where the contestants were limited to a half dozen dry fly patterns, the renegade would be the first fly I would put in my box. It would be followed by an elk hair caddises, stimulators, grasshoppers, royal coachmen, a parachute Adams, and maybe an ant pattern. You can find renegades, though, in many fly-fishing shops. Shaya believes that renegades with a lot of green sparkle in them are better than the darker ones. For this reason, she takes peacock feathers to our local fly-tying expert in Columbia Falls, Montana, Bob Arens, who uses them to tie renegades for her.

Barry invited us over to his house the next morning for a breakfast of the brook trout that he had kept. We had a wonderful meal prepared by his wife before we parted company. We met Barry several times more on our trips to Warren. We learned how to navigate the rough roads to the various dredge ponds in our rental vehicles and spent many wonderful days catching trout. We also visited the Winter Inn on many more occasions. One time we had dinner there on a Friday night—the place was jammed. Where all the people came from I have no idea. Warren is located in one of the most remote areas of the West that you can drive to. But somehow people found their way there. Today, the place is still there but it has changed names: It is now the "Baum Shelter." I would like to return to Warren at least one more time before I hang up my fly rod.

The Winter Inn, Warren, Idaho. AUTHOR'S COLLECTION.

Fishing Silver Springs:
Following in Hemingway's Footsteps (Or Should I Say Waders?)

Somewhere along the line in my extensive research on places to wet a line, I discovered the iconic Silver Creek in central Idaho. What makes Silver Creek iconic? According to Mike McKenna who wrote a nice article about it, "Fishing Idaho's Iconic Silver Creek," for the Nature Conservancy in partnership with Visit Idaho, several things make it special: Big and wild fish, clean and protected views, amazing aquatic insect hatches, and its proximity to Sun Valley. But there is something much bigger than all of that which makes it iconic: Its most famous fisherperson, "Papa" Ernest Hemingway. The famous author first visited Silver Springs in 1939 and fell in love with it. Writing to his son, Jack, he vowed that they would fish it together the following year, which they did. In fact, the Hemingways had a lifelong connection with Silver Springs. Years later, Jack convinced the Nature Conservancy to purchase the property when it came up for sale. In 1976, the Conservancy preserved 476 acres of the Springs and surrounding area. Hemingway's last home was in nearby Ketchum, Idaho.

How could I pass up a chance to follow in the footsteps of another great fly fisher? So, during one of our sojourns to Idaho, we booked a motel in Ketchum and hired a guide to take us fishing on Silver Creek. Now, in all seriousness, I do not presume that I am in the same category with Hemingway either as a writer or a fly fisher. But it turned out that we were to have one thing in common. On Ernest's first expedition on Silver Springs, he saw big trout rising everywhere. He cast and cast but got skunked—and so did I. In fact, it turned out to be one of the most frustrating days that I would ever spend on the water. For openers, the guide was a jerk. I have not said much about guides in this epistle, but they generally could be said to fall into two camps: Those who are willing to work with their clients based on the clients' skill levels and those who spend their time screaming at the clients when they are not able to perform up to the guide's expectations. This outing took place relatively early our fly-fishing history, so neither of us really had the expertise we needed to fish Spring Creek. Yes, there were trout everywhere. Big pods of them racing below the surface. I had trouble seeing them and when I did see them I had difficulty making a decent cast. Worse still, we were in float tubes and my ancient waders started leaking. We had to take a time out to go back to the guide's house so I could rent a pair of waders. The guide was not a happy camper, and neither was I. But that's not the end of the story. Shaya, of course, was with me. Rather than instructing the both of us, he decided early on that she was hopeless, so he sent her off in exile to fish by herself. You can guess what happened. I got skunked, but my wife did not. About an hour into the expedition, she hooked a big trout. We could hear her hollering that she had one on the line. By the time that the guide and I made it over to her in our float tubes, she had already netted a two-pound rainbow.

Hemingway, of course, returned to Silver Creek for many years and I am sure he figured out how to catch the trout. Sadly, this was the only time we fished Silver Springs. I wonder if I were to return now, would I do any better than the first time? I would like to think so. The trip turned out not to be a total bust for me, though. Shaya and I spent a few pleasant days fishing the nearby Big Wood River where we had pretty good luck.

The Hot Springs of Idaho: Be Bear (Bare) Aware

One of the most wonderful things about Idaho outside of the fishing is the hot springs. They are all over the place. So, when it was time for us to take a break from fishing, we would head out to refresh ourselves in the thermal waters. Some of the hot springs are developed; others are back in the woods. Our favorite developed one is Burgdorf Hot Springs located north of McCall. To describe Burgdorf as "rustic" would be an understatement. It is the site of an old mining development and some of the cabins that miners lived in are still standing. In fact, you can rent one. The hot springs themselves are encased in wood with pebbles on the bottom. It's a wonderful place to meet people while soaking. One of the famous remote hot springs is Jerry Johnson Hot Springs in the Clearwater National Forest. It's about a two-mile, round-trip hike to the springs. Before visiting some of the remote hot springs, it's always a good idea to check local customs: Some of them are clothing optional.

Our favorite hot springs, though, were the local ones that not many people knew about. One of them was located fifteen miles south of where we used to camp on the South Fork of the Salmon River. You knew you were there because someone had tied a ribbon to a tree. If another vehicle were parked in front of the tree, you waited until the people using the hot springs had left. After tent camping for several days, Shaya and I decided that it was time to visit the hot springs. So, early in the morning we drove the fifteen miles down the road. We were in luck: No one was there. We walked about fifty yards down the trail to the springs. Boy scouts had tapped the water coming out of the hillside so that it ran out of a pipe into the pools below. The wonderful thing about this hot spring was it is on the banks of the ice cold South Fork. So, after soaking in the steaming water for fifteen minutes or so, one could screw up one's courage and plunge into the river to cool off.

When we arrived at the pools, we took off our clothes knowing that we would have the place to ourselves—or so we thought. This day we had taken biodegradable soap with us to wash off. It was almond scented— a big mistake in retrospect. That very morning Shaya had complained that we had not seen any wildlife on our vacation. This was about to change. As we were washing our hair, I happened to look to my left. There was a very large cinnamon-colored bear heading straight for us. The bear was no more than fifty feet away. I tapped Shaya on the shoulder and said, "Look who is coming." She looked and saw the bear. "Oh my God, what are we going to do?" she cried, while trying to hide in the shallow pool. We were bare and the bear was coming. And our vehicle was fifty yards up a hill.

I did the only thing I could think of. I jumped up and clapped my hands. The bear looked up, startled. It turned around and ran off into the woods. We were saved. The moral of the story? Be careful about complaining that you have not seen any wildlife, and don't take almond scented soap with you to the hot springs.

Big "Cut bows" on the Clark Fork
(or When is a Rainbow not a Rainbow?)

Although Idaho is a hot springs mecca, Montana has some wonderful hot springs also. On one of our sojourns through the West, we decided to visit one of Montana's best—Quinn's Hot Springs Resort. Quinn's is located in a remote area of Montana on the Clark's Fork River about seventy miles west of Missoula. After pitching our tent in a campsite a few miles down the road, we arose one morning, packed up our swimming outfits and headed to Quinn's for a relaxing day soaking in their pools. It is a wonderful place, and we have been back many times since. Although located in a remote area, Quinn's has a gourmet restaurant and hosts a Baroque music festival every spring. But luxuriating in the hot springs was not our only reason for visiting this area. The Clark Fork, a mighty river that flows for over 300 miles through Idaho and Montana, has excellent trout fishing today. This has not always been the case, though. By the 1980s, the Clark Fork's water quality had gone into a steep decline for a number of reasons but importantly by the degradation caused by over a century of mining activity. In the 1990s, the Clark Fork Superfund site was created. In 2008, the Milltown Dam was removed, and tons and tons of metal sediments removed. Now the Clark Fork has a bright future.

I knew that the Clark Fork has the reputation of being a tough proposition to fish—the trout can be persnickety—but we were excited about trying our luck. So, one evening after we done soaking at Quinn's, we headed down to the Clark Fork, strung up our fly rods, put on our waders, waded out into the water and began casting. Nothing. As it began to get dark, though, I noticed some activity out towards the middle of the river. Some trout were definitely slurping up flies. I also saw some small brownish flies floating by. So, I pulled out my fly box and found a few that closely resembled the flies in the river. Shaya had some similar flies too. I had an advantage over my wife, though: Because I am about eight inches taller, I was able to wade about twenty feet farther out into the river than she. I managed to put the fly right in front of a rising trout. Much to my amazement, the trout slurped it up. I set the hook and the battle was on. Whatever it was on the end of my line, it was big. It took off down the river and I had no choice in the current but to chase after it. Finally, the fish began to tire. I managed to bring it to net. What a beauty! It appeared to be a cutthroat trout that easily weighed four pounds. I returned the fish to the river and headed back up to where I had hooked it. Trout were still feeding there. A few minutes later, I hooked another and landed another big one. Then the action was over.

As you know, one of the great joys of having a good day on the river is telling everyone about it. So, the next morning, I could not wait to find some unsuspecting person (victim?) with whom to share my fishing story. As we headed west on Montana Highway 135 towards the town of St. Regis, I spied a sign for a resort. "Let's check it out," I said to Shaya.

After several minutes of winding around gravel roads, we found it. We met the owner who showed us around the lovely resort that he had built. It turned out that he was a professor at the University of Idaho and a guide of many years on the Clark Fork. After I had regaled him with my tale of catching the large trout the day before, he asked me a simple question, "Did they jump?"

I thought about it for a second and said, "No."

"Hum," he replied. "Probably cut bows."

This was the first time that I had ever heard of a fish called a cut bow. He went on to explain that cut bows are a cross between a rainbow trout and a cutthroat trout.

Although rainbow trout are the most popular gamefish in Montana today, the fact is that they were native to only a small part of the state in the upper Kootenai drainage. According to the Montana Field Guide, beginning in the 1880s, they were introduced from numerous hatchery stocks into virtually every suitable habitat in the state. Like so many of man's efforts to improve upon nature, introducing rainbows into Montana's lakes and rivers had an unintended consequence—and it was not a good one. It turns out that rainbows and cutthroat trout can interbreed. While some hybridization had occurred between rainbows and cutthroats in places where their native ranges overlapped, the introduction of non-native rainbows greatly increased the rate. The result has been the decline of genetically pure cutthroat trout in Montana (and other western states) through "genetic pollution" to the point where they are considered endangered. Were the two big trout I caught on the Clark Fork years ago cutthroats or cut bows? The truth is that I will never know. And the same is true for many of the trout I would catch on many of Montana's rivers in later years. It's almost impossible to tell the two apart.

Having let the proverbial cat out of the bag, state of Montana and national park officials are now in a desperate race to try to save genetically pure westslope cutthroat trout. How are they attempting to do this? The answer is by first "treating" a lake or stream that have cut bows in them with

Westslope cutthroat trout. BIODIVERSITY HERITAGE LIBRARY.

the poison rotenone and then restocking them with pure-bred cutthroats. The pure-bred cutthroats must be secured from remote bodies of water that are somehow cut off from the cut bows. Ironically, one of the best places to find them is on the South Fork of the Flathead River above the thirty-eight-mile-long Hungry Horse Reservoir created by the construction of the Hungry Horse Dam in the 1950s. The reservoir provides hydro-electric power for the region, but in my humble opinion it should never have been built. Damming up the South Fork destroyed more than thirty miles of a wild and scenic river that was part of the insane "reclamation" mania that swept the United States for decades. Building the dam, however, would have a positive consequence that no one could have foreseen at the time: It provided an insurmountable barrier between the cut bows and the genetically pure cutthroats. So, now state of Montana and national park personnel go deep into the heart of the Bob Marshall Wilderness to catch and bring back to civilization the precious cargo of cutthroats. How do they procure the cutties? They employ a variety of methods but one of them is by fly fishing! That's right. They hike back into the "Bob" with fly rods in hand to catch small cutties that will later be released into streams and lakes. (I must say that I have applied for a job doing this several times, but so far have been turned down in spite of my sterling qualifications. Go figure!)

The poisoning of the lakes and streams itself has become controversial. Many local Montanans are vociferously opposed to it. I am ambivalent about it myself. I do not have any problem with the authorities trying to preserve genetically pure cutthroat trout, but sometimes they seem to go overboard. Here's a case in point. Handkerchief Lake is located thirty-eight miles up the Hungry Horse Reservoir west-side road. To access it, your turn off the west-side road and drive a few miles up a gravel road until you reach some primitive campsites. Shaya and I have never been able to fish Handkerchief because at our advanced age the trail through the woods down to the shore is too rough for us to negotiate with our inflatable kayak. However, I have talked to several expert fly fishers who fished it over the years. They raved about the size of the grayling they brought to net: The fish often exceeded two pounds. At one point, the state record for a grayling came from Handkerchief Lake weighing in at over three pounds.

But then the authorities discovered that the cutthroat trout that also inhabited the lake were no longer genetically pure. So, in spite of an enormous outcry from the local population of fisherpersons, the lake was poisoned with rotenone several years ago and restocked with arctic grayling and purebred cutties. The jury is still out on whether this restocking will be successful. Last summer, Shaya and I drove up to the lake to check things out (I am still trying to figure out how to get a watercraft down to the shore). We met a family camping at the lake that had recently moved from Texas to Montana (Imagine that!). I saw that they had some fishing rods with them, so naturally I asked whether they had any luck. They replied that they had not done much angling but that a few fly fishers had showed up the day before with float tubes. They added that the fly fishers had headed down to where Graves Creek enters the lake and had caught of bunch of small fish, maybe six inches long, that the new Montanans thought were smallmouth bass. I gave them a mini-lecture (hey, I am former professor) explaining that the fish were not bass but the rare and highly sought after arctic grayling. They seemed unimpressed by my piscatorial knowledge, so we said goodbye and headed back home. It's only been a few years since the grayling restocking began. Maybe in three or four years more, the grayling will grow to the size of the jumbo fish that inhabited the lake before it was poisoned, but who knows? Perhaps this is one lake the authorities should have left alone.

Arctic grayling. BIODIVERSITY HERITAGE LIBRARY.

The stocking of Lake Trout in Northwest Montana's Flathead Lake has been an even bigger disaster than the introduction of rainbow trout. If you have not been to Montana, Flathead Lake is enormous. At thirty miles long and seventeen miles wide, it's the biggest freshwater lake west of the Mississippi in the Lower 48 states. In an attempt to improve upon nature, a number of non-native fish were introduced into Flathead Lake, including the lake trout in 1905. They did not really thrive until 1968 when the Mysis shrimp (also introduced) reached Flathead. The lake trout feasted on the shrimp, and their population soared. Today, according to an excellent article by Eric Wagner, "The Great Flathead Fish Fiasco" that appeared in the *High Country News* (February 3, 2014), there are an estimated 1.6 million lake trout in Flathead Lake. This in itself would not be a bad thing if it were not for the impact that the population explosion had on the native bull trout population. The bull trout is a char and is native to Canada and the western United States. Compared to other similar species found in the West, they grow quite large. Four or five pounds would be about the average, but they can get much bigger: Some are over ten pounds. They prefer high mountainous areas where snowfields and glaciers are present and mainly live in deep pools of rivers and in cold lakes. They have been classified since 1999 as "threatened" under the Endangered Species Act. This is due to a number of factors, including the introduction of non-native lake trout into their habitat, climate change and a decline in water quality. The bull trout population in Flathead Lake had already been hit hard by dams and logging, but the lake trout were a new kind of threat, devouring young bull trout and outcompeting adults. By 1996, estimates were that just 1,300 bull trout survived in the lake. They have made something of a comeback since then with perhaps as many as 5,000 remaining today. Worse still, the lake trout migrated up the Flathead River system to spawn where they found their way into many of Glacier National Park's big lakes, decimating the bull trout population. Efforts to remove the lake trout have been largely ineffective. In eight of twelve lakes, the bull trout are now functionally extinct.

What have the authorities done to rectify this disaster? That becomes complicated because two authorities manage Flathead Lake: The northern part of the lake is controlled by Montana Fish, Wildlife & Parks; the southern half by the Confederated Salish and Kootenai Tribes Fisheries Program. The native Americans want the lake trout gone; the Montana fish people are more ambivalent. The reason for the ambivalence is simple: The enormous lake trout population has spawned (hah, hah) a healthy sport fishing industry. Dozens of charter boats ply the waters of Flathead Lake angling for lake trout A full day on the lake (nine hours) will cost you around $800. In order to mollify the Salish and Kootenai tribes, semiannual fishing derbies called "Mack Days" have been organized to reduce the lake trout population. The number of lake trout that are brought to net annually by boats plying the lake during "Mack Days" is impressive—around 50,000. Individual boats often catch well more than a hundred lake trout in a single day. The native Americans have more ambitious plans. Several years ago, they released a draft plan to reduce lake trout abundance by as much as seventy-five percent over the next fifty years through a variety of methods. The Montana state authorities, though, backed out of what was supposed to be a collaborative process and published a series of objections in local newspapers after the plan was released. I guess the Montana fish authorities can afford to be purists when it comes to saving the western cutthroat trout from disappearing because there's no big lobby opposing it. But when a profitable sport fishing industry squawks about saving the bull trout at the expense of the lake trout, it's a different story.

Bull trout. WIKIMEDIA COMMONS

Onward to Montana

The Bob Marshall Wilderness: Burned Out!

While I was working for the American Association of University Professors during our years in Champaign-Urbana (1980–1985), I met Bob McClellan, who worked for AAUP's national staff. When Bob wasn't working for AAUP, he taught American history at Northern Michigan University in the Upper Peninsula. Unlike me, Bob was a real outdoorsman. When we took breaks from visiting colleges and university faculties together, we would talk about the wilderness. Bob had been to Montana many times and had gone backpacking in the Bob Marshall Wilderness Area several times—in the winter. The "Bob," as it is known, is named after the conservationist and legendary hiker, Bob Marshall, co-founder of the Wilderness Society. Marshall was the guiding force behind getting the USDA Forest Service to preserve large areas as roadless wilderness. The BMWA was enshrined in law by the Wilderness Act of 1964. The "Bob" consists of over one million acres and runs for sixty miles along the Continental Divide. Today, as back in 1964, there are only two ways to get into the BMWA: On foot or on horseback. From my conversations with Bob, I made a hard mental note to remember the "Bob," thinking I would like to visit it someday.

After we moved to Austin many of our summer trips would be to Idaho, but Montana had always been in the picture. In fact, in 1982 (six years before we moved to Texas), the Zucker family drove all the way from

Champaign-Urbana to Glacier National Park. We did this trip with our good friends, Bob and Bobbie Rosenthal, and their two children. Each family traveled in its own vehicle. We kept in touch using CB radios as we cruised down the highways. It was a fabulous trip. The West still had the feel of being wild back then. Bozeman was a sleepy college town with a few restaurants, some bars, and several fly-fishing shops. Kalispell struck me at the time as a frontier town.

After we moved to Austin, I began planning a trip into the "Bob." I learned that located within the BMWA is perhaps the finest cutthroat trout fishery in the United States—the South Fork of the Flathead River. I also learned that to get to the best fishing spots in the "Bob," would take a Herculean effort by my standards. We would have to hire an outfitter to take us there on horseback. So, I began researching outfitters and finally settled on Mark and Janis Moss, owners of Salmon Fork Outfitters, headquartered in Columbia Falls.

Mark and Janis operated a base camp on the banks of the South Fork twenty miles from the departure point at Spotted Bear, fifty-five miles south of Hungry Horse. Twenty miles on a horse! For a person who grew up in Chicago and whose main exposure to horses was watching them race at Arlington Park with my father, it seemed a daunting task. But I began practicing. Fortunately, because Austin is located on the edge of the Texas Hill Country, there were plenty of riding stables where I could rent a horse. I started out riding for an hour or so and then for two hours or more. But the trip into the Salmon Fork base camp would take about eight hours. Mark and Janis assured me there were places where I could dismount and walk for a mile or two. And I was encouraged by the video Salmon Fork sent me: It showed horses walking calmly along the banks of the river. (More about that later.) We flew to Boise about two weeks before our trip scheduled for late July and worked our way towards Columbia Falls. The night before Marlene from the Salmon Fork staff was to meet us, I was feeling really ill. To this day, I don't know what was wrong with me: It may have been merely a bad case of the jitters or maybe I was suffering from a real malady. In any case, with Shaya's encouragement, I screwed up my courage and off we went in the morning to meet Marlene at Laurie's Deli in Columbia Falls. We threw our gear into her truck and started on the long road to Spotted Bear along the massive Hungry Horse reservoir. We were to stay overnight at some cabins at Spotted Bear before starting out on our trek in the morning.

It so happened that the day we departed with Marlene marked the 100th anniversary of the Spotted Bear Ranger Station. Festivities were planned for the afternoon. We arrived just in time to enjoy a picnic lunch and to watch a mule train carrying antique fire-fighting equipment. Shaya and I were having a wonderful time. Then we overheard a conversation on a CB radio between a ranger at the station and a ranger out in the "Bob." The ranger was reporting a fire that apparently had been started by careless campers. People seemed concerned but not overly alarmed. When the picnic was over, we headed back to our cabins, had dinner and settled in for the night.

Nothing could have prepared us for what we would see when we awoke in the morning. As we stepped out of the cabin, we were shocked to see a massive cloud of smoke arising from the "Bob" It looked like the whole world was on fire. A little while later, Mark and Janis held a meeting with the dozen or so folks scheduled to go to the base camp. The news was grim. "There's no way we can get there," Mark informed the group, "The trails are closed." He offered to take us on another route through the "Bob" that was still open, but we would not be fishing on the South Fork. We both quickly decided that we did not want to do that. So, instead of giving us a "rain check," Mark gave us a "fire check." We could do the trip the following year.

I had been practicing horseback riding for months and now the trip was off. I remember feeling like an athlete who has trained for a big meet for months only to find out at the last moment that it has been cancelled. We took the long ride back to Columbia Falls with Marlene who kindly let us pitch our tent in her back yard for the night. What were we going to do? We were both feeling dejected, to say the least. But then in the morning our mood changed. After all, we had our camping gear with us. There could be worse fates than having ten days to explore the wilderness of Montana. Like so many things in life, something that at the time seemed disastrous turned out to have a silver lining. I had maps of Montana, of course, and a travel guide. We decided to head out to one of the most remote areas of the United States: The Yaak Valley.

The sparsely populated Yaak Valley is located along the Yaak River and has become known in recent years due to the writings of Rick Bass, a petroleum geologist by training who is now a well-known author. The Yaak is yet another one of Montana's gems. The tiny community of Yaak is home to the "Dirty Shame Saloon," one of those wonderful places that you occasionally stumble upon in the West. Shaya and I stopped in saloon one night to have hamburgers and a few beers for dinner. We had a great time visiting with locals. The Yaak is for people whom do not want much to do with "civilization." Many, if not most of them, live off the grid. The winters are brutal. The Yaak has good fly fishing too, though Shaya and I did not have much luck there. During our ten days, we explored many other wonderful areas in northwest Montana, including the beautiful Ten Lakes Wilderness Study Area bordering Canada. To get to the campgrounds on Big Therriault and Little Therriault Lakes, you take a left turn near the hamlet of Fortine and drive twenty-six miles up a narrow, winding mountain road. On several occasions after I retired, we took our small T@B camper up the road and we have also tent camped there. There's good fishing in many of the lakes in Ten Lakes area. When our time was up, we headed back to Boise and flew home, determined to return to the "Bob" the following year.

Return to the "Bob": A Once-in-a-Lifetime Fly-Fishing Experience

The delay in our trip to the Bob Marshall gave me another full year to practice horseback riding, though the idea of the twenty-mile ride still gave me the jitters. I also planned as carefully as I could to be prepared for fly fishing the South Fork. Shaya and I were somewhat better than beginning fly fishers by this time, but there were still a lot of western dry flies with which we were unfamiliar. Mark and Janis had a list of recommended flies that I purchased. This time we flew directly from Austin to Kalispell. Marlene picked up us at our motel the next morning and we headed out once again up to Spotted Bear. We were in luck. The weather was beautiful and no forest fires to speak of. In the morning, Mark and Janis loaded up the fifteen or so guests' packs on their mule train.

We mounted our horses and were off on our twenty mile, eight hour ride. Now Mark and Janis, who are now retired, are wonderful people. But the video they sent to us of the horses walking calmly along the shore of the South Fork towards the base camp in no way prepared us for the reality of the trip. Surprise, surprise! The "Bob" is extremely mountainous. Before I knew it, we were headed up precarious paths where one false step by our horse could send horse and rider over the side of the cliff. Of course, the horses were well trained and had been over the trails dozens if not hundreds of times. But this was little comfort for a tenderfoot like me. It did not help my confidence when Mark announced somewhere along in the journey that we would have to take a detour because a pack horse had fallen off the regular trail to its death the week before and grizzly bears were busily eating it. And then about three hours into the trip, I saw several horses in front of me begin to snort and buck up. One of the horses had stepped on a hornets' nest on the ground. The angry hornets had begun stinging the horses. Panic among the horses quickly spread backwards to where I was—about eighth in line. My horse began rearing up. "Holy shit," I thought, "I am going to get thrown." Somehow I managed to hold on. We trotted past the hornets. The day wore on. We stopped for lunch. When we hit relatively flat areas, Janis allowed me to dismount and walk for a few miles, leading my horse behind me. This helped enormously. Finally, we saw the base camp a few hundred yards in front of us. We made it! I dismounted feeling plenty sore but happy that I had endured the long ride. For the next few days, I would walk bow-legged. After a hearty dinner, we were shown to our tent where we drifted off to sleep.

The next morning after breakfast Shaya and I rigged up fly fishing rods and headed for the river. The South Fork in the "Bob" is perfect for wade fishing. It averages maybe fifty yards across and is not deep in most places.

Although you could hire a guide through Salmon Fork, the prevailing wisdom was that a guide is not needed because the fishing is so good. Each fly fisher headed out along the river on his or her own. There's plenty of river to explore, so Shaya and I never felt crowded. Most of our compatriots on this trip were much more experienced fly fishers than we. On the first day, while they caught a ton of beautiful cuts (all catch and release), we struggled to catch maybe three or four fish each. I remember walking back to camp feeling despondent, thinking that we were not going to catch many trout and that the trip was going to be a bust. But as the days passed, we caught on. While fishing on the Henry's Fork requires great skill in matching the hatch and presenting the fly perfectly, fishing on any of the stems of the Flathead does not. We learned almost intuitively when it looked like a good time to try an elk hair caddis, an ant pattern, royal coachmen, humpy or a stimulator. We also knew that if one fly were not working after ten minutes or so, tie on a different fly. And it helped that the fish were hungry. The number of trout we were catching each day climbed into the double digits. Most were in the ten to fourteen inch range, but we landed several that were bigger. Meanwhile, the more experienced anglers on the trip were averaging around thirty fish per day.

Time out here for a word about fly-fishing etiquette. There are two ways that a fly fisher can access the South Fork inside the boundaries of the "Bob." The first one is the way we did it: A long, grueling trip on horseback both ways. The other is to ride a horse into the "Bob" but float out on a raft. We encountered several rafting fly fishers during our time on the South Fork. This was not generally a problem. We would wave to them from where we were fishing on the shore or in the river as they floated by. However, one day Shaya and I were standing on the banks of a pool: A hatch was on and we were catching one beautiful cut after another. Along came a couple of rafts. Darned if they did not stop in the pool we were fishing and begin to cast. The South Fork is over ninety miles long, so it is not as if they were not going to find another place where the fish were biting. To this day, I am pissed about what they did— and by the fact that

I did not ask them to move along. Perhaps the guides felt that their clients had a higher priority than we because they were in a raft.

On one day of the expedition, the group took a side trip to fish for bull trout on Big Salmon Lake. This meant another serious horseback ride— seven miles each way. But what the heck, by now I was starting to feel like a real mountain man. Of course, any bull trout we caught would be returned immediately to the water. We arrived before noon, but alas the best spot to fish from shore had already been taken by several young men who had hiked into the lake. They had a field day catching several large bull trout. Alas, our group did not do well. I think the entire Salmon Fork party maybe caught a total of two or three fish. Shaya and I struck out. Oh well, it was a beautiful day, nonetheless.

Where have All the Pretty Horses Gone?

Our time at the base camp was drawing to a close. On the last day of the journey, Mark and Janis informed the fly fishers that pursuant to Montana regulations, each person was allowed to keep two trout under twelve inches long. We were to have a fish fry that evening. Shaya and I marched off to the river eager to do our part for the fish fry. Darned if we did not have a problem: All the fish we were catching that morning were over twelve inches. It was as if the little ones knew that their lives were on the line and ran for cover. What a problem! Finally, we each hooked two that were the right size and we headed back to camp. After a tasty fish fry that evening, Shaya and I went walked back to our tent to get a good night's sleep before they long ride back to Spotted Bear the next day.

When we awoke in the morning, we were in for big surprise: About half of Salmon Fork's horses were gone! Now, what I knew about caring for horses and mules on a backcountry trip you could put in a thimble. I did know that the person in charge of caring for livestock is called a "wrangler." I also knew that Salmon Fork's beloved lead wrangler had tragically passed away the winter before. So, maybe the absence of this trusted wrangler had something to do with what had happened. I have learned that it is common on these trips not to hobble the horses so that they can graze during the long evenings in order to keep up their strength. (You will learn more about this on our second trip into the "Bob.") Apparently, at some point in the evening, another pack trip headed back to Spotted Bear had passed by. Some of Salmon Fork's horses decided to up and join the group. Perhaps they were trying to shirk the long walk back to the corral with a heavy tourist on their back. I have to admit that I was slow to understand the import of the missing horses: We could not all get back to Spotted Bear together. Mark and Janis had to ask for volunteers to remain for two more days. With a great of juggling, they could accommodate everyone except for two guests. It so happened that everyone had to get back to town except for the two of us. After about five minutes of deliberation, Shaya and I informed Mark and Janis that since someone had make the great sacrifice, we would stay behind. Two more days of fly fishing on the South Fork. What a horrible fate! In fact, Shaya caught her largest cutthroat of the trip on the last day of our layover.

Why I Hate Bed and Breakfasts

The ride back to Spotted Bear with Mark leading the way was long and tiring. The temperature had soared into the eighties and the trail was dusty. To make matters worse, Mark had to stop at a corral along the way to make arrangements with a wrangler for a future trip. Finally, we crossed the last creek and the end of the trip was at hand—except for the fifty-five-mile ride in Mark's vehicle back to civilization.

When we arrived in Columbia Falls, we had to find a place to stay. I consulted my tourist guide (this was long before the Internet). Thinking we should pamper ourselves after the exhausting trip, I made a reservation for two nights at what appeared to be a delightful B&B just outside the town of Big Fork. I won't mention the name of this B&B because it is still in business. When we arrived, we discovered it was delightful. The decor was beautiful with lots of antiques; our room was large and comfortable. Then I noticed all the rules posted on the wall—there were at least a dozen of them. Shaya almost immediately got into big trouble because she took the wrong color towels down to the pool. Our hostess chewed her out for taking the green towels, which were for the bathroom. Hadn't Shaya read the rules? She was supposed to take the brown towels. Then there was the matter of breakfast. Since it was quite an elaborate affair, the hostess served it only once—at 8:30 or 9 am if I remember correctly. What I do remember is waking up the next morning around 6:30 as hungry as a bear that has just come out of hibernation. I looked at my watch with great consternation realizing that I had about two hours to wait before I could get something to eat. To say that I was grumpy would be putting it mildly. Finally, the appointed hour came, and we dined. The breakfast was fine, but we both agreed that we did not want to wait around the next morning for another one. So, we asked our hostess if we get something to eat earlier in the morning because we wanted to get on the road. Oh my God! Our hostess was bent out of shape. She finally agreed to set out some coffee and rolls for us around seven, but cautioned us not to make any noise so as not to disturb the other guests. The next morning, we tiptoed down the stairs, had our coffee and rolls and departed.

In fact, one of my favorite stories by the outdoor humorist, Patrick F. McManus, is entitled "Bed and Breakfast." In this story, one of McManus's buddies talks him into staying at an upscale B&B on their next outdoor adventure. When they arrive at the B&B, their host meets them at the door in a blue blazer and immediately rattles off a long list of rules they must follow. Pat is dismayed and tries to figure out a way to get out of staying at the place. Finally, he convinces the host that his muddy hunting dogs must stay with him in his room. The host will have nothing to do with this arrangement and Pat is off the hook. He and his buddy find a cabin down the road where the hostess greets them heartily while carrying a couple of sloshing minnow buckets up from the lake. My kind of place, Pat concludes, as they check in. I had the good fortune to meet Pat at a book-signing event in Austin. Sadly, he passed away several years ago.

Up To Alaska

Sea Kayaking in Prince William Sound

In the summer of 2000, Shaya and I journeyed to Alaska on a three-week adventuring trip to Alaska. We did not plan this primarily as a fishing trip, but, of course, we planned to do some angling while were there. In July 2007, we flew first from Austin to Anchorage, where we spent several days exploring the city and surrounding area. Then we flew to Valdez where we rendezvoused with a sea kayaking company for a five-day trip exploring Prince William Sound. I do not pretend to be anything like a world-class adventurer, but I have to admit this was hair-raising trip. The information we received from the kayak company omitted important details—much like Salmon Fork Outfitters had on our first rip into the "Bob.

For example, only during the kayak company's briefing the night before our departure did we learn that if our kayak tipped over in the sound, we were mostly certainly going to become hypothermic and die. It only takes a minute or two in the frigid water before you are a goner. Of course, the company used huge two-man sea kayaks; but the water, as we were to learn, can become mighty rough in the sound. On day one, a large motorboat took our group of only four people and our guide about fifteen miles up the sound ,where we were dropped off on shore. Then it was *bon voyage*. Following our guide, we all kayaked to an island where we spent the night.

Now, this kind of camping is not for the faint of heart. We learned during our briefing that there would be no toilet paper. If you had to go number two, why, you used some wet rocks and then some dry rocks that you found on the beach. And then there was the weather. One of the main reasons why so few people live in Alaska is because the weather is horrendous. It rains in Valdez almost 200 days per year with an average annual rainfall of about seventy inches. Shaya and I were in Valdez for three days before we saw the sun. Only then did we learn that gorgeous mountains ring the city. We were lucky on our trip, though, because the weather was relatively good with highs in the upper fifties during the day and the lower forties at night. Still, after one grueling day of paddling on the sound, I found myself shivering uncontrollably in our tent. Our guide put warm rocks in my sleeping bag to keep me from going into hypothermia. Then there were the incessant mosquitoes and black flies while we were on shore. They were maddening, though I have to admit not as bad as we had experienced in Minnesota. Fortunately, I had somehow found room to stow a container of box wine in our kayak. Shaya said to me before we left, "Why are you bringing that?" But after a few days out on the sound, as soon as we reached shore, everyone would shout, "Where's the wine?"

On day two, we were supposed to cross the sound to explore the other side. Our expedition made it about halfway across, when we encountered a wall of massive chunks of floating ice. Wisely, our guide decided that we should turn around. So, we paddled to a beautiful bay, which we explored before returning to our original campsite. It was indeed gorgeous. Sea otters popped up all around us. After an hour or so, it was time to head back to camp. The only problem was that the wind had picked up, and so had the waves. As we rounded the point before our bay, the guide yelled, "paddle as hard as you can!" He obviously did not like the way things looked. Just then I heard Shaya gasp. A giant sea lion had surfaced right next to our kayak and scared the hell out of her. Finally, we were in calm water. The guide pulled his kayak up on shore but fell in the water as he was getting out. Fortunately, he was okay. He was the only one of the five of us who fell in during the expedition. The next day the massive chunks of ice were still there, so the guide radioed the motorboat as it passed by. The captain picked us up and we were ferried across the sound to the other shore where we spent two glorious but challenging days exploring Shoup Bay State Marine Park.

Then it was time to head back to Valdez. The only problem was on our last night, we were having trouble finding a place to camp. As we headed back out of the bay, the guide found a place on shore, but there were far too many signs of grizzly bears in the area for him to feel comfortable camping there. We got back in the kayaks and finally found a spit of land just barely big enough for our tents. There was only one problem: The guide wasn't sure that the land would be there when high tide hit. Fortunately, the other man on the trip (his name escapes me after all these years) was a scientist. He had a GPS with him and was able to determine that we probably would be okay. Still, as a safety precaution, we lashed the kayaks together so that they would not float away if we found ourselves submerged in the middle of the night. We all slept nervously but

Out on the spit: Prince William Sound, Alaska. AUTHOR'S COLLECTION.

remained dry. The next day we did the nine-mile paddle back to Valdez where Shaya and I rested up for a day before embarking on the next leg of our adventure.

From Valdez to Wrangel-Saint Elias National Park

Many years ago, we saw a wonderful TV documentary on Alaska's spectacular Wrangel-St. Elias National Park & Preserve. I decided early in planning our Alaskan adventure that we needed to visit this park. According to the National Park Service, Wrangel-St. Elias is six times the size of Yellowstone and is the largest park in the United States. Mt. St. Elias, at 18,008 feet, is the second highest peak in the U.S. The Nabesna Glacier, at approximately fifty-three miles, is the longest valley glacier in North America and the world's longest interior glacier. Although it's possible to drive from Valdez to the town of McCarthy, which sits just outside the park's boundaries, I thought it would be fun to experience a flight with an Alaskan bush pilot. So, I made reservations for us to fly from Valdez to McCarthy where after a short ride from the airport, we would check in at the historic Kennicott lodge.

We met our bush pilot, who flew for Wrangell Mountain Air, at the Valdez airport at 10 am for the short flight to McCarthy. We learned that he been a part owner of an upscale Alaska fishing lodge for many years, but grew tired of dealing with his partners and decided to cash in his chips for a simpler life. We also learned that he had graduated from Northwestern University, where I had received my Ph.D. After pleasantries had been exchanged, he informed us that he had some bad news. "Folks," he said, "I just learned that the fueling station at the airport does not open today until 3 pm." He added that he thought he had enough fuel to get to McCarthy but did not want to take any chances. We were incredulous. Okay, the Valdez airport is not exactly O'Hare International but a lot of planes land and take off from there. Our pilot had a plan, though. He knew that he had enough fuel to make it to the airport at Chitina, a tiny town on the Copper River about halfway between Valdez on McCarthy. Once we were there, he was pretty sure he could find more fuel for his plane. So, we loaded our gear onto the small plane, climbed on board and took off. The scenery between Valdez and Chitina was breathtakingly beautiful as we flew along a valley with spectacular mountains and glaciers on each side of us. After about a half an hour, we could see the Chitina landing strip below us. We landed and taxied up to a small wooden shack that served as the "terminal." Our pilot asked us to standby as he looked for fuel. So, we sat on the stoop of the shack and waited. By this time, we were seriously wondering what we had gotten ourselves into. Several large metal barrels were scattered around the airport. He proceeded to begin testing each barrel by dipping a long metal rod in it to see if it contained the right kind of fuel for his plane.

The town of Chitina, located on the Copper River, has an interested interesting history. Athabascans lived in the vicinity for centuries before Europeans arrived. The discovery of copper in the area around 1900 led to a rush of prospectors and homesteaders. The arrival of the Northwestern Railway and the fact that Chitina is located on the Copper River enabled the town to flourish. By 1914, it had five hotels, a general store, restaurants, bars, dance halls and a movie theatre. But when the copper played out in the 1930s, Chitina became a virtual ghost town. When we made our brief visit to the town, the population had made something of a recovery, sporting a population of maybe a hundred people. Current activity revolves around fishing for the plentiful salmon with dip nets and fishwheels during the summer months.

After a long wait, our pilot reported that he had been unable to ascertain if any of the fuel in the barrels would work in his plane. But not to worry. He got out his phone and called headquarters at Wrangel Mountain Air. The boss said she would fly out from McCarthy in a plane and "rescue" us. About an hour later, we saw her plane in the distance. Within ten minutes or so it had landed. She got out of the plane holding a big gas can. Within a matter of minutes, our original plane had been refueled. But we flew with her the rest of the way to McCarthy. Today, by the way, Wrangel Mountain Air no longer seems to fly between Valdez and McCarthy. You have to drive to Chitina to take the short flight to McCarthy. Oh well.

After a short bus ride from McCarthy, we checked into Kennicott Glacier Lodge located in the historic town of Kennicott. This town was once the site of a huge copper mining enterprise. In 1911, the first train-load of copper was headed to Cordova before being shipped to Tacoma for smelting. The National Park Service states that from 1911 to 1938, nearly $200 million worth of copper was extracted from the mountains and the mill town where the ore was processed. At the peak of its operation, approximately 300 people worked in the town and about 200 to 300 in the mines. Kennicott was a self-contained company town. By the late 1920s, however, high-grade ore was diminishing and the town—like so many other mining towns—fell into oblivion. In 1986, the National Park Service acquired many of Kennicott's significant buildings and lands and today the whole shebang is designated as a National Historic Landmark.

It is considered to be the best remaining example of early 20th century copper mining. The lodge itself was delightful. Meals were served family style at long tables, so we had the opportunity to meet other guests and swap adventures. Alas, the fishing in the immediate area was pretty non-existent, but we had a wonderful time exploring the historic buildings, trekking on a glacier and hiking in the mountains to an old mine. In the planning the trip, I had assured Shaya that it would start out with more strenuous activities but then things would taper off. By the time we were finished with our Kennicott activities, Shaya began asking me, "When is the easy part of this vacation coming?"

After the Kennicott adventure, we flew back to Valdez and then on to Anchorage. With a day to spare before heading down to the Kenai peninsula to do some fishing, we rented a car early one morning and made a wonderful one-day, eight-hour, round-trip drive from Anchorage to Denali National Park. We wished we had had more time to spend exploring the park, but Alaska is so big that you have to make decisions. We were lucky, though, because the day we went the sky was crystal clear. We had wonderful views of glorious Mt. Denali, the highest peak in North America with a summit elevation of 20,310 feet. We met many people on our vacation who had been to the park for several days but never saw the peak because of cloudy weather. If we were to return to Alaska, I would plan to spend a minimum of three days at Denali.

Fly Fishing the Kenai Peninsula:
Do Salmon Strike Your Fly or Are You "Snagging" Them?

But now it was time to go fishing—except there were complications. In order to explain the complications, I need to back up. As part of planning the Alaskan adventure, I devoted several hours to reviewing online the qualifications of Alaskan fishing guides. I contacted one that had consistently high marks and booked him for several days of fishing. Based on my recollections, he did not ask for any money at the time, which was several months before our departure date. Several weeks passed with no follow-up from him. I started to get nervous, so I sent him another email or called him—I don't remember which. Many more days passed with no word. I remember standing on the first tee of the Plum Creek golf course south of Austin when my cell phone rang. It was the guide. He informed me that since I had not sent him a deposit, he had cancelled my reservation and booked other clients. I was out of luck. There was no apology or even an offer to find another guide for me. I was dumbstruck. Okay, it's entirely possible that Charles screwed up; maybe I was supposed to send in a deposit by a certain date and missed it. But I don't think so. What really puzzled me at the time was why this guy did not simply contact me again and say, "Charles, I need a deposit within the next few days or I am going to have cancel your trip." Of course, I would have sent it off immediately. But one thing I learned on our vacation is that a lot of Alaskans are up there for a reason. They are a self-selecting group who are highly individualistic and often quite eccentric. My guess is that a better gig came along for this guide, so he thought the hell with us. In his defense, maybe he had a lot of people who booked trips with him who never sent any money.

We headed down the Kenai Peninsula in our rented automobile to go fishing sans a guide. I figured we would find one once we arrived in the area. By the way, since there are only about five highways in all of Alaska, if you have never gone, you may be surprised by the traffic. The last thing

I expected driving in Alaska was traffic jams. But there we were traveling down Highway 1 at a snail's pace behind dozens of RVs that had made the arduous 1,300-mile -plus drive up the Alcan Highway from the Lower 48 to Alaska. Finally, we reached the lodge where we had reservations. A few hours later, we were having a drink at the bar before having dinner at one of the local eating establishment; naturally the patrons were carrying on a lively discussion of fishing. I allowed that we needed a guide. A gentleman turned to me and said, "I know a good one" and he gave me the guide's telephone number. I called the guide, who said he was free for the next two days, so I booked him.

The next morning, he arrived at our lodge—a pleasant young man towing a drift boat behind his truck. We climbed into the truck and set out to fish the Kenai River for Sockeye Salmon that were running at the time. After a short drive, we arrived at a huge lake. He put the boat in the water, we got in and he began rowing across the lake. At this point, nothing struck me as unusual because we had never been fishing before in this neck of the woods. But I remember that as he rowed farther and farther out on to the lake, we both started to grow nervous. The weather was threatening, and the lake looked foreboding. We began wondering what would happen if a storm were to kick up. It turned out that were traversing Skilak Lake, one of the largest lakes on the Kenai Peninsula. It is fifteen miles long, up to four miles wide and it is indeed treacherous. Why were we crossing it? Because the Kenai River flows out of the other side of the lake. Finally, after more than hour row, we reached the river. Within a few minutes, we started to see fisherpersons dotting the shoreline about every two-hundred yards or so. Most of them had gotten to the Kenai the same way we did—by boat. But Shaya and I noticed that all of these boats had motors on them. It was then we learned that our guide's motor had broken down about a week before. Rather than taking time out in the middle of the salmon run to drive to Anchorage to have the motor repaired, which would have taken three or four days, he decided to row his clients everywhere. Of course, we were exasperated. But we were there, so it was time to start fishing.

Now, maybe you have been to Alaska and had a wonderful time fishing, but this was not my cup of tea. I think expectations had a lot to do with my disappointment. When planning our trip, I imagined Shaya and myself standing in the proverbial gin-clear river somewhere deep in the Alaskan wilderness with nary another fisherperson in sight. This was combat fishing, pure and simple. The guide landed the boat at a favorable looking spot, we climbed ashore and he rigged up our large fly-fishing rods with big wet flies. We began casting for the salmon.

There's a certain technique to fishing these wet flies for the salmon, which after all these years I only vaguely remember. The sockeyes were there in huge numbers. However, as any student of fishing knows, spawning salmon stop feeding as soon as they reach fresh water. Their only interest is in reproducing. So, why would one hit your wet fly? The theory is that spawning males will strike wet flies because they are all riled up by sex hormones—thus, they will lash out at anything that gets in their way. Females, the theory adds, may strike a fly because they are protecting the eggs they are carrying. There's another theory, though: The salmon are not really striking your fly—they are being snagged. That is, the river is so thick with fish that if you make enough casts, a hapless salmon will get hooked just by opening its mouth. Take your pick. My guess is that it is some of both.

Did we catch any sockeyes? You bet. Shaya caught way more than I did. If memory serves, she landed around six and I brought around three to shore. These fish put up a tremendous battle. I lost several of them. As the day wore, we talked to other fly fishers on who wandered by the spot where we were angling. The experts had this down to a science. God knows how many they landed. I remember talking to a fly fisher who hooked and landed an eight-pound sockeye as nonchalantly while we chatted as if he were fishing for eight-inch bluegills in a pond back in the Lower 48. Of course, we kept our limit of sockeyes, had them smoked and frozen and then shipped back to us at home. They were delicious. At the end of the day, we rowed back across Skilak. The next day we fished another river for Dolly Vardens but only caught a few. The problem was that there were so many sockeyes running that the Dolly Vardens had made themselves scarce.

This ended our Alaskan fishing experience. You may ask, "Charles, why did you not go halibut fishing or book a trip at a remote lodge?"

Regarding the halibut fishing, I thought seriously about going. But the idea of racing from the port in Homer out into the ocean for thirty miles then bouncing around in the boat for several hours bottom fishing left me cold. I have to admit in retrospect, though, Shaya and I should have tried it. We may not get another opportunity to go halibut fishing. Passing on fly fishing at a remote lodge was an easier decision. It was just too darned expensive. At the time, we simply did not have the $5,000 or more to spend for a week of fishing. And even if we did have the bread, we would have taken a pass. I think all fisherpersons do their own informal cost-benefit analysis when planning a fishing trip. Shaya and I dearly love to fish, but we have limits on how much we are willing to pay for a week of angling. If we were to travel to Alaska again, what would I do differently? Well, for one thing, I would make sure any guide I booked got our deposit on time; for another, I would love to pursue the arctic grayling. Maybe we will go again. Who knows?

Sockeye salmon. U.S. FISH AND WILDLIFE SERVICE.

CHAPTER VII

Retirement and T@B Adventures

Buying the T@B

The year 2007 was another momentous one for Shaya and me. In August of that year, I retired. Our boys had been out of college for many years by that time and thankfully were gainfully employed. Shaya had been diagnosed with breast cancer many years before but was now cancer free—thanks to the wonderful treatment she had received at MD Anderson in Houston. Having cancer is a life-changing experience. She was anxious for me to retire so that we could begin traveling more. I was now sixty-three years old. Although I still found my job as the director of the Texas Faculty Association interesting, I was definitely suffering from burn-out. Recruiting members was a large part of what my job entailed, so for many weeks in the fall and again in the spring, I departed on Monday morning for the week to visit different college campuses around Texas—a state that is as large as France. Thank God for Southwest Airlines! I quickly discovered that flying was the way to go when striking out for places like El Paso or Edinburg. But I also had to do a tremendous amount of driving to schools that were closer at hand like Southwest Texas State (San Marcos) and UT-Dallas. Lugging my briefcase stuffed with membership materials around a campus from one academic building to another became increasingly taxing, as was staying in motels and eating in restaurants every day.

Then there was the matter of the Texas Legislature. I did have previous lobbying experience from my years working for AAUP in Illinois. But Texas was a whole different ball game. In many ways, it was like lobbying in a foreign nation. (Well, native Texans do proudly point out that Texas was a foreign nation from 1836 to 1845.) The culture was extremely different from what I knew as a Yankee from Chicago. Northerners like to get things done in a hurry. You set up a meeting, discuss the business at hand and hopefully reach an agreement. Texans, on the other hand, tend to engage in a lot more polite banter before anything of substance is discussed. It takes a while to get down to "bidness." But fortunately for me, most legislators expected a lobbyist representing college professors to be somewhat "different." So, I did okay. Over the years, I developed strong relationships with many legislators. But then around 2003, the Texas Legislature started to change. It became more openly ideological with conservative Republicans sweeping into power. Now, I do not mean to offend you if you are a conservative, but I depended heavily on the support of the more progressive legislators such as Rep. Wilhelmina Delco, Rep. Irma Rangel, and Sen. Gonzalo Barrientos. With people like that gone, I could not get anything done. It was most frustrating.

Shortly after I had retired, Shaya and I were on our way back from Houston to Austin when she spotted a cute little camper in an RV dealership along the Interstate. We stopped to look at it. It turned out to be a T@B—an ultra-light teardrop-shaped camper about sixteen feet long. Of course, I was totally opposed to buying a camper. As a person who suffers from high anxiety, I could not imagine myself towing a trailer of any kind behind my vehicle. But you know how that goes. In the fall of 2007, we drove up to Vogt RV Center in Ft. Worth to purchase a T@B. We ordered a turquoise-blue-and-cream-colored one equipped with a combination air conditioner/heat pump, refrigerator, stove, and a dining table that folds down so that you can put cushions on top of it to make a bed. Alas, the T@B did not come with a toilet. I had a tow hitch and electrical wiring for towing added to my brand new Toyota Highlander. One month later, we picked up the T@B. The two-hundred-mile ride back to Austin was quite a nerve-wracking adventure. Somewhere along the way, a bale of hay flew out of the truck in front of us. I was terrified, what with the camper behind the Toyota. I hit the brakes gently and the bale of hay went flying over the Toyota. We will never know if it also hit the T@B, but fortunately it did cause us any problems. Finally, we were back home, and I thankfully parked the Highlander and T@B in front of our house. Over the years, I would develop a love/hate relationship with this darling little camper.

Onward to Idaho, Wyoming, and Montana

The summer of 2008 was our first extended tour of the West towing the T@B. By this time the Austin Angler had closed up but a first-rate fly-fishing and hunting shop, Sportsman's Finest, had opened on Bee Caves Road about twenty minutes from where we lived. Before our journey began, I had stopped by Sportsman's Finest. Some of the crew from the Austin Angler now worked there, including Joe Robertson, who had given me my first fly-fishing lesson. I picked Joe's mind about where to go out West, especially in Wyoming, where he had guided for many years. Joe said, "Make sure you go the Snowy Mountains," (also known as the Medicine Bow National Forest). He also mentioned the town of Saratoga on the North Fork of the Platte River located just west of the Snowy Mountains. So, we loaded up the Highlander, hitched up the T@B, and early one morning in June, Shaya, our Old English Sheepdog Sarie, and I headed out on the road. I soon grew somewhat accustomed to pulling the T@B. I learned to be careful when stopping at service stations to make sure I did not hit a pump, and when we stopped to eat to make sure that we did not get hemmed in by other vehicles. I also learned to request a campsite near the bathroom facilities when making a reservation at an RV campground.

On our previous trips out West while I was still gainfully employed, our travels were limited to two or three weeks of vacation time. Now, I am not complaining. One thing about working for a teachers' organization is that although the pay may not be great, the vacation time is generous. But now that I had retired, we could spend the whole summer exploring—that is, if we could ever make it out of the Lone Star State. Texas is,

The T@B, Aspenwood Campground, Blackfeet Indian Reservation. AUTHOR'S COLLECTION.

as advertised, a huge: In fact, it has about the same number of square miles as France. The distance from Austin to Texline, which borders New Mexico, is 616 miles. As a new trailer hauler, I was reluctant to go more than sixty miles per hour, which meant that at the end of day one, we only reached Lubbock. By day two, we had managed to reach Colorado. By day three, we were in Wyoming. That is when I began to notice that the T@B's refrigerator was not cooling. In retrospect, I should have said the hell with it and gone to a big box store to buy a cooler to keep our food in. But, of course, on the T@B's maiden voyage, we wanted everything working perfectly. What I did not know then (and would only discover more than a year later) was the outfit that had done the work in Austin to connect the Highlander's electric system to the T@B's seven-way plug did not know what the hell they were doing. A piece of advice here: If you ever need to have a traitor hooked up to your tow vehicle, go to U-Haul. They know what they are doing.

So, we stopped in an RV facility in Casper to see if we get the problem fixed. The kindly gentleman at the repair shop informed me that it would be about three weeks before they could look at it since the RV season was in full swing. They were swamped. But he knew a good RV repair shop across town that could get to it right away. The next morning, I pulled into the shop and asked the technician if he could wire the T@B properly. He said he could. But as the day wore on, I began to have my doubts. About five hours later, he was finished. I paid the bill, which, if memory serves was exorbitant, and I departed. The good news was that the refrigerator was now cooling. I would only come to know the bad news about the work that he had done later in our trip.

After leaving Casper, we drove to Laramie and then took Highway 130 towards our destination. Joe was right about the Snowy Mountains—they are gorgeous and well worth visiting even if you never toss a fly into a lake or stream. Though it has been many years since we have visited this wonderful area, I have fond memories of it. Lake Marie and Mirror Lake are both beautiful lakes over ten thousand feet above sea level. We found a campsite for the evening and the next morning headed out to try our luck fly fishing. We caught some small rainbow trout on dry flies at a lake that had been heavily stocked with rainbow. But the fishing in the Snowy Mountains was just mediocre, so after a few days we headed for the town of Saratoga.

Saratoga is a lovely tourist town. It is home to the Hobo Hot Springs. The springs are wonderful place to relax but they are not for the faint hearted: When you wade into the water, you will know what it is like to be a lobster thrown into the proverbial boiling pot! The North Fork of the Platte River runs right through town. This is a blue-ribbon trout stream noted for its large cutthroat, rainbow, and brown trout. The weather when we arrived was, unfortunately, in the mid-eighties: Too hot to leave our Old English Sheepdog, Sarie, in the Highlander while we went on a fishing expedition. So, Shaya and Sarie relaxed in a park beside the river while I tried my luck. Alas, after a few hours, I had not caught a single fish. I finally did have one take a swipe at a wet fly, but I didn't hook it. I talked to another fly fisher who had been on the river for several hours who also had been skunked. He had fished the Platte many times before, so presumably knew what he was doing. Not everyone got skunked though. I talked to a man in the Orvis fly shop who had had a wonderful time the day before fishing with a guide on the Platte. He was thrilled in particular by the large brown trout that had rushed after the gaudy streamers he was tossing. The North Platte is one of those rivers I wish I had had the opportunity to fish properly. I'd like to give the Platte another chance someday—perhaps hiring a guide from the Orvis shop.

We departed from Saratoga and headed for the wild and beautiful Big Horn Mountains in north-central Wyoming. The website for the Bighorn Mountains describes the area as "an outdoor paradise filled with recreational opportunities including hunting, fishing, camping, hiking . . ." and more. Congress established the Cloud Peak Wilderness, which is located in the Big Horn National Forest, in 1984. It is a wonderful remote area but one that, alas, I have never had the chance to explore. We pulled into Deer Park Campground for the evening. The next morning, we hooked up the T@B and headed up Highway 16, the Cloud Peak Skyway, into the mountains. We found a nice campsite at the Lost Cabin campground twenty-nine miles west of Buffalo, but I must tell you that trying to back the T@B into the narrow campsite proved to be one of the most harrowing experiences of my life! Up until then, we had been lucky. We had somehow managed mostly to stay in RV campgrounds where we were directed to a "pull through" campsite for the T@B. No problem. But the Lost Cabin campsite was a different matter altogether. What I had learned about the T@B by then is that although it is a joy to tow, it is a son-of-a gun to back up. It turns out that short campers like the T@B jackknife in a New York minute when backing up. This is something I had not counted on. Our futile efforts to back the T@B into the campsite soon drew a crowd of campers who shouted advice and encouragement. Some even offered to park the T@B for us. After about a half an hour, Shaya finally parked the T@B. To this day, I suffer from "T@B anxiety" when it comes time to back the T@B into a site. This remains Shaya's job. Campers that are motorized so that you just pull directly into a site have a big advantage over the T@B in terms of parking, though they have other shortcomings.

The next morning, we fished a small stream in a meadow not far from our campground. This proved to be unlike any fly fishing I had done up to that point. If memory serves, it was already July, but we were way up in the mountains, so the spring thaw was just underway. We could actually see the trout racing around in the winding stream, which was no more than eight feet wide in most places and only a few feet deep. We managed to find a few pools where we both caught an assortment of small brook trout on dry flies. An added attraction was a cow moose that appeared with her twin calves perhaps a hundred feet away. During our Minnesota adventures, we had seen many a moose, but those sightings were almost always from the safety of a fishing boat or while we were in a vehicle. Fortunately, another fisherman was close by who warned us to keep our distance from the mom less she should decide to charge us.

Disaster on the West Tensleep

The following day we went exploring and discovered the West Tensleep River about twenty miles west of our Lost Cabin campsite. We followed a gravel road that ran parallel to the river for several miles before we found a place to park the Highlander. We donned our fishing gear and waded into the river. On my very first cast, a nice-sized brookie took a vicious swipe at my fly. Always a good sign. Over the next few hours, I caught a half-dozen or more brook trout in the ten- to twelve-inch category on dry flies. Shaya did not do as well but also caught a few. We waded back to the Highlander, stowed our fishing gear and prepared to head back to our campsite. It was a wonderful day of fishing. We were excited about the prospect of returning to the river the following day to try our luck. Little did we know what was in store for us.

We started up the Highlander and headed back towards the Cloud Peak Skyway. About one hundred yards down, the motor died. No amount of tinkering could get it started again. I later learned that the mechanic who had "fixed" the T@B's electrical problem wired it in such a way as it caused the Highlander's electrical system to short out. We were stuck in a remote area, and it was beginning to get dark. I raised the Highlander's hood to let anyone who might come along know that we were in distress. About forty-five minutes later, a pickup truck headed towards the highway came along. The vehicle pulled over. It was a husband and wife who graciously agreed to take the two of us and our very large Old English

Sheep Dog, Sophie, in the pickup back to Buffalo. The couple dropped us off at a motel where I had time that evening to contact a towing company.

In the morning, a tow truck with an enormous flatbed trailer showed up at our motel. The driver (whose name I do not remember after all these years) proved to be a character. Shaya and I hopped in his cab and we began the steep drive up the Cloud Peak Skyway wondering if he would be able get his gigantic big into the Lost Cabin campground to "rescue" the T@B before heading up to the West Tensleep to tow the Highlander. He maneuvered the rig into the campground with remarkable skill and within fifteen minutes, or so, the T@B was on the flatbed trailer. Then it was off to the West Tensleep River Road where he hooked up our vehicle to the back of the flatbed. We were soon barreling down the Skyway towards Buffalo. We had noticed that our driver had a cast on his arm; naturally, we asked him what had happened. I turned out that he had been out hunting prong horned sheep on his three-wheeler and had had an accident. The three-wheeler had flipped over, breaking his arm.

Heading back to town, the driver told us about an accident that occurred on the Skyway the day before—one that made our mishap pale in comparison. The grade heading down Highway 16 to Buffalo is extremely steep. An elderly couple in their Winnebago motor home neglected to do a brake check on their way down the Highway. Somewhere along the way, the Winnebago's brakes failed, apparently from overheating. They soon found themselves heading towards town at a breakneck speed without any way to stop. They managed to alert the state police on their CB radio and a unit was soon following them down the road. But there was nothing the police could do. The couple was doomed. Highway 16 tees with Main Street in downtown Buffalo. Unable to stop, the couple crashed into an insurance agency building. One of the two was killed (I do not remember which one) and the other seriously injured. Fortunately, the Winnebago struck the insurance agency and not the ice cream stand next door, so no one else was hurt. The ice cream stand, by the way, is still there.

The tow truck dropped the T@B off at the RV campground and then proceeded with the Highlander to the Toyota dealership in Sheridan where the Highlander was rewired. (I later learned from the Princess Craft RV in Georgetown, Texas, that the Toyota repair shop had not wired it correctly either, but at least our tow vehicle remained operational for the remainder of our trip.) We rented a car in Buffalo, drove it up to Sheridan, picked up the Highlander and then drove both vehicles back to Buffalo. We dropped off the rental car, hitched up the T@B and were on the road again. Whew!

Hyalite Creek: I Get a Fishing Lesson

Our next stop was in the Absaroka-Beartooth Mountains, where we camped on Hyalite Creek about fifteen miles outside of Bozeman. We had stopped in Bozeman about twenty years before on our epic journey to Glacier National Park with our friends, Bob and Bobbie Rosenthal. Bozeman had changed so much since we had last been there that we were shocked. (More about that later.) Hyalite Creek received moderate fishing pressure even then, but it had a nice campground. Moreover, we had camped somewhere in the vicinity with the Rosenthals, and I wondered if I could find the campsite. I had fond memories of arising early one morning, taking my spinning reel and some worms and catching some nice brook trout, which we later had for breakfast. A few years ago, I had the satisfaction of finding that campsite which, it turned out, is on the Hyalite Creek Road above Hyalite Reservoir. After finding the campsite, Shaya and I took an enjoyable short hike to Hyalite Falls.

The fishing on Hyalite Creek was slow but I learned an important lesson by watching an expert woman fly fisher who we met at the campground. Hyalite Creek is not big—maybe fifty feet across and eminently wadable in summer. This woman walked down the middle of the creek casting her fly just a short distance in front of her. The fly floated then slowly down the river without any drag. Bang! She had a trout on her line and then another one. I soon was following her lead. When I am able, this is my preferred method of fly fishing today. Over the years, it has worked extremely well for me while wade fishing the North Fork of the Flathead River. In short, I do not cast unless it is necessary. I toss the fly out a few yards and let it float down the river. If there's nothing doing, I wade out a few more steps into deep water and repeat the process. Still nothing doing, I move down the river perhaps ten yards or so. Today, I see so many fly fishers who seemingly have become enamored of casting. They make multiple unnecessary false casts before actually throwing the fly. Perhaps they watched Robert Redford's classic movie, *A River Runs Through It,* too many times. You can't catch a trout while the fly is in the air. Of course, if you are fishing on a good-sized river or from a boat, then casting is a must; or, if you are casting towards a rising fish. But much of the time when I am prospecting for trout, it's just a matter of letting the fly drift over a fish and hoping that it will rise to the surface to inhale the fly.

Our next stop with the T@B in Montana was in the Ten Lakes Wilderness Study Area just outside of Eureka. You may remember that we first explored this gorgeous area after our first trip into the Bob Marshall got cancelled because of the huge forest fire. We camped in our tent during that visit and did well fishing for cutthroat trout in Little Therriault Lake. (The fishing this time, though, on Little Therriault this time would be slow.) We took the T@B the twenty-eight miles up the twisting mountain road to get to the campsite. In fact, we would make this trip several times with the T@B, but I would not risk it again because for many miles it's a one-lane road. If a big RV were headed down the road, I do not know what I would have done. Fortunately, we were lucky and made it okay on our trips. The last time we visited the Ten Lakes area, we took our tent camping gear and had a great time, though we almost froze to death since it was in late September and the temperature at night plummeted down to below freezing. There's wonderful hiking in the Ten Lakes area to the various lakes. Unfortunately, many of them are now beyond our hiking range. One beautiful hike we were able to manage last time was to Bluebird Lake—about four-and-a-half miles round-trip. We also we found an incredible bonanza of huckleberries on that hike ready for the picking. (More about Montana's love affair with the huckleberry later.)

Our next stop was on the North Fork of the Flathead River near the remote hamlet of Polebridge. I had it from several reliable sources that the North Fork was teeming with cutthroat in the six- to ten-inch category.

At this point in my evolution as a Western fly fisherperson, though, I still had much to learn. The river looked promising, but I only caught a few trout. I did talk to one spin fisherman who told me that he had caught over sixty trout using a sinking silver lure down in deep holes. A few years later, the North Fork would become my favorite trout stream in northwestern Montana. However, it would take several trips to the river to learn what time of year to fish it and where to fish it before I would start catching trout in abundance. I would also discover that they were not all six to ten inchers either—the North Fork also holds some big trout.

Fishing the Spotted Bear River: Heaven on Earth

After more than a month of roughing it in the tiny T@B, it was time for Shaya, our Old English Sheepdog Sarie, and me to take a break. So, we rented a historic cabin for ten days at Abbott Valley Homestead located on Spotted Bear Road just outside of Martin City. Abbott Valley is a wonderful place where we stayed on several occasions during our tours of Montana. Two of the many cabins on the grounds are historic—over one hundred years old.

Abbott Valley also put us within striking distance of the Spotted Bear River, which I had wanted to fish since our trip into the "Bob" several years before. (Well, "Striking distance" is a relative term because the river was a good fifty miles up the East Side Road from Abbott Valley.) The Spotted Bear is actually a tributary of the South Fork of the Flathead, but you don't need to backpack or get on a horse to fish it. A decent gravel road runs along it for eight miles with several places to pull off. I have been fortunate to fish many beautiful rivers in my lifetime, but there's something about the Spotted Bear that would make me put it at the top of my list. Perhaps it's that fact that it is a heavily braided river that is constantly changing. Or maybe it's the deep pools that you encounter along the way. I have often thought if I were ever to make it to the Pearly Gates and the Good Lord were to say to me, "Charles you have a led far from exemplary life, but it was good enough. Welcome to Heaven." I might reply, "With all due respect, Almighty One, I would just as soon pass on Heaven. If it's okay with you, may I have my favorite fly rod and a handful of flies back?

I would be happy if you would just let me wonder along the Spotted Bear for eternity."

The trout were biting on our first day on the Spotted Bear. We each caught several beautiful cutthroats on dry flies as we wandered along the river. Darned if I did not manage to lose a big cut that was lurking in one of the pools. I made the mistake of trying to net the fish before it was through fighting. On the second day, conditions had changed: It was hot and clear. The temperature would reach ninety-eight degrees back in Kalispell by mid-afternoon. After a few hours of fishing in our waders, we were hot. So, we took a break. Stripping down to our skivvies, we jumped into an ice-cold pool where we had caught some nice trout just a few minutes before. After lunch, I decided to head downstream to fish some big pools, while Shaya fished upstream. The fish were not cooperating until I decided to fish a dry fly with a trailing wet fly. As soon as I added the wet fly to my line, I started catching nice sized trout—in fact, one after another. But here's the funny thing—I hooked almost all of them on the dry fly! Go figure. Did the wet fly slow down the dry fly's drift just enough that the trout made lethargic by the hot weather went after it? Or, perhaps it was just a coincidence—that is, I would have started catching fish without the wet fly. Only the trout knew the answer and they were not talking. A few hours later, I met up with Shaya. She had landed a beauty—a cutthroat that easily weighed two pounds.

Over the years, we would make many more enjoyable trips to fish the Spotted Bear. On one of them, we drove many miles down the road that parallels the river and then hiked in a half a mile to fish some pools. We could see some huge trout lurking on the bottom but no matter what we tried, they turned up their noses at our offerings. Some of them were undoubtedly bull trout. It was maddening. About an hour after we arrived, two gentlemen fly fishers showed up. They did not stop to fish the pools where we were but headed upstream at a lively clip. Later that evening, I talked to them at the Spotted Bear campground where we had pitched our tent. They told us they had had a terrific day. They said that there was another series of pools farther up the river. They had caught most of their trout on dry flies fished in the film just below the surface. They were experts; I was (and remain) a novice compared to them. Of course, I fully intended for us to return to that spot and try the pools where they had such good luck. But we never made it. Given our advanced ages now, it seems unlikely that we ever will.

Good Fishing on the Salmon River

Our best trout fishing on our maiden voyage with the T@B was yet to come. We checked out of our cabin at Abbott Valley and headed for Stanley, Idaho, gateway to the Sawtooth Mountains. We had not been in Idaho for several years and were reminded almost instantly how incredibly gorgeous this state is. If you love rivers, mountains, white-water rafting and hot springs, this is the place for you. The Salmon, Payette, Lochsa, and Clearwater Rivers are among our favorites. After a long drive, we pulled the T@B into a campsite on the Salmon about ten miles northeast of Stanley. The next morning, we stopped by the local Orvis store where the proprietor recommended that we try some caddis flies. We bought a handful and headed out to the river. Insects were hatching all over the place—always a good sign—and the trout were snatching them up. We started catching rainbows in the ten- to twelve-inch range. As an added bonus, I caught several nice sized mountain white fish on dry flies. Some fly fishers turn up their noses at mountain whitefish, but I enjoy catching them: They always put up a good battle. The second day on the Salmon was even better. I landed a cutthroat that easily weighed two pounds. and we must have caught thirty trout in total. In retrospect, we wondered why we did not stay a day or two longer since fast action on a trout stream is all too rare. We would fish the same spot several times in later years but did not have the same luck.

It was time to head home. We fished our way back through Wyoming but without much luck. It may have been the time of year. I have learned that mid-to-late August is generally a poor time for trout fishing the West—unless perhaps you are hiking up to a mountain lake. Sadly, after getting skunked in the Jackson Hole area, we packed away our fly rods for the last time.

The Economic Collapse of 2008
and the "Fly-Fishing Shop Recovery Act"

In the fall of 2008, the stock market crashed as a result of bad invest-ments by firms such as Merrill Lynch and Lehman brothers, both of whom declared bankruptcy. With the world economy tottering on the verge of total collapse, in February 2009, the Obama administration and Congress passed the American Recovery and Reinvestment Act—a gigantic stimulus package that would eventually total dump some $831 billion into the economy. Nicknamed the "Recovery Act," its primary objective was to save existing jobs and create new ones as soon as possible. Other objectives were to provide temporary relief programs for those most affected by the recession and invest in infrastructure, education, health, and renewable energy. A little-known part of this package was intended to provide relief to affected fly-fishing shops: "The Fly Fishing Shop Recovery Amendment." Although sadly no federal funds were ever allocated to this amendment, the Zuckers took it upon themselves as their patriotic duty to implement this worthwhile amendment as best they could. During our tours of the West in the T@B from 2009 to 2011, we contributed to the recovery of dozens of fly-fishing shops through frequent and often-excessive purchases of fly-fishing paraphernalia, including but not limited to dry flies, wet flies, tippet material, leaders, vests, waders, boots, rods, reels, gunk, t-shirts, and more. God knows how many fly-fishing shops might have had to close their doors if were not for us! (Shaya informs me that this practice has not stopped even with the recovery of the economy.) Although the official Recovery Act saved the day for many families and businesses, I did have one bone to pick with it. You see, an enormous amount of money from the Recovery Act went into road construction and a lot of that construction took place in the western states. This meant that the Zucker's efforts to get from, let's say, Saratoga to Thermopolis, Wyoming, might take five hours instead of four. And the interruptions were frequent. I took to swearing a blue streak every time we had to stop.

CHAPTER VIII

Putting Down Roots in Northwestern Montana

Buying the "Lodge" on Lynnewood Drive

We continued our explorations of the West during the summers of 2009 and 2010. Although we continued to have a wonderful time, I began to realize that I could not spend the remainder of my retirement summers in the T@B. First, there's the issue of RV parks—most of them are pretty dreadful places. We generally found ourselves crammed into to a spot with giant RVs parked no more than fifteen feet away on each side of us. The people who occupy these rigs, which can easily cost over a half million dollars, typically don't care where they are parked for the night because they are in self-contained cocoons complete with giant TVs, sofas, king-sized beds, washers and dryers, showers, toilets, and so on. Folks often stopped by our campsite to look at the T@B and proclaim it to be "so cute." But they weren't living in it. For me, the biggest drawback to the T@B has always been its lack of a toilet. As an elderly male, I normally have to get up at night to pee. This means making mad dash to the restroom that may be as far as fifty yards away. Although I soon learned to use a "pee bottle" when the restroom was too far away or the weather too inclement, peeing in a bottle standing behind the T@B in a well-lit campground is not always a good solution. On one occasion, in an RV campground just outside of Missoula, I nearly knocked myself out when I hit my head on a flowerpot on the way back to the T@B. In an RV campground outside of Yellowstone, I slipped and fell on an icy wood walk during a blizzard. "Dry camping" was usually better because I could usually find some cover in the woods, but not always.

Then there's the issue of noise. I am a very noise-sensitive person. The T@B's three-way refrigerator drove me nuts for years. The problem was a fan that would cycle on and off every time the fridge started to heat up. Finally, after about eight years, it broke. What a relief! We bought a decent cooler and now keep our food in it outside the camper. The fridge has been repurposed as a storage place for bread, etc. On our "shake down" voyage with the T@B, we also had a horrendous problem with a carbon monoxide detector that malfunctioned. It took us several hours to figure out how to turn the blasted thing off. Also, RVing for long periods of time is not conducive to a healthy lifestyle. Yes, we did some hiking, etc., but we spent far too much time driving and sitting around in RV campgrounds. A summer home would allow us much more time to recreate. (Okay, enough grousing about the T@B. It spite of all my complaints, it has provided Shaya and me with a great deal of enjoyment and still does.)

I had some retirement funds squirreled away from my years of teaching at Carroll College, and it was amazing how much money had accumulated over the span of thirty years. Every so often, my annuity company, TIAA-CREF, would end me a statement. This was always gratifying. But one day it occurred to me that I was not getting any real enjoyment out of looking at the financial statements. Why not invest some of the funds in a humble fishing cottage in the West? It took me a while to persuade Shaya to buy into the scheme. I argued that we could still use the T@B for adventures but that we would now have a "base camp" we could return to instead of staying in expensive motels or lodges when we had reaching our limit of "T@Bing." And we could begin to acquire toys to enjoy in the outdoors.

My first thought was to look for a place around McCall, Idaho. McCall had for years been one of our favorite places: It had a beautiful lake, a nice golf course and gorgeous scenery in the mountains just outside of town. The one thing it did not have, though, was outstanding fishing. I had by learned by now on our travels through the West that Montana's trout fishing was superior to what we had experienced in Idaho. So, our attention turned to the area in northwest Montana near Glacier National Park. Finding a summer home would turn out to be an ordeal in its own right that would take two years. Fortunately, we found a wonderful real estate agent, Vicki, who was interested in protecting our interest as well as making a sale. I finally realized that we would never find the ideal property in our price range. We would have to compromise.

So, in the spring of 2011, I sent an email to Vicki saying that we would do an Internet search and select several properties before flying up to Kalispell. After looking at them, we would make a decision as to which was the best one to fit our needs—much like what happens on the TV show, *House Hunters*. All winter I had been looking at a home a few miles outside of Columbia Falls that was in a small subdivision. We originally thought that we would like to be in a cabin out in the woods, but as time went on we changed our minds. First, there was the issue of driving a long way into town every time we needed something; second, we might have difficulty finding someone to look after the summer home when we were back in Texas; finally, we began to realize that we were, after all, city folks who liked the idea of being just a few minutes away from grocery stores, restaurants, and so forth. When we walked into the house on Lynnewood Drive, it was as beautiful as it had looked on the Internet. A few days later, we made an offer; after a bit of haggling, the owners accepted. We closed on June 23—the day our grandson Max was born.

Buying a summer home fifteen miles from Glacier National Park and just a few miles outside of Columbia Falls turned out to be one of the best decisions we have ever made. Our neighbors in Lynnewood Estates, for the most part, have been wonderful. We have also made several good friends who live in the Flathead Valley. And now that we had a home base with a large two-car garage we could begin to accumulate toys: We purchased bikes, two hard-shell kayaks and hiking equipment. But my most important purchase was an inflatable two-person kayak made by Saturn.

It's about fourteen feet long and has a removable skeg, which means that it tracks well on big lakes. Why more fisherpersons in the West don't use inflatable kayaks is a mystery to me. It sure beats fishing from a float tube or a pontoon boat. Also, the fact that my "humble fishing cottage" turned out to be a three-bedroom home meant that we could invite friends and family to visit. Our only requirement (outside of no smoking) is that if they do not agree to go fishing within twenty-four hours of their arrival, they may be asked to leave.

Now that we were solidly planted in northwest Montana, I could begin to explore much more intensively the area's rivers and lakes.

The North Fork of the Flathead:
"The Last Best Place" to Fly Fish on Earth

Montanans like to say that their state is "the Last Best Place." And with good reason. It has an incredible abundance of natural beauty and, unlike Texas, access to public land is protected with the same ferocity as a mother grizzly bear protecting a cub. What's more, Montana is sparsely popu-lated—it just reached the one million mark a few years ago. One of the reasons that we chose the Flathead Valley area is because it was even more remote than other popular areas of the state such as Bozeman. As I men-tioned earlier, we had previously visited the tiny hamlet of Polebridge, home of the legendary Polebridge Mercantile, which is famous for its huckleberry bear claws, on our first ill-fated attempt at horseback riding into the "Bob" with Salmon Fork Outfitters. I remember thinking at the time that we were at the end of civilization. (Now, of course, I know bet-ter. It's the "backyard" for natives of Columbia Falls and the surrounding towns.) We had also tried our luck briefly fly fishing for trout in the North Fork but with little success. But now we were more experienced fly fishers.

The North Fork of the Flathead was to become our special "Last Best Place" to fish for trout in Montana for several reasons. First, it is drop-dead gorgeous. Okay, I know that I raved about the Spotted Bear earlier on in this missive, but the North Fork is just as beautiful. The North Fork originates in British Columbia and flows some one hundred and fifty-three miles before joining the main stem of the Flathead River north of Columbia Falls. Once it reaches the border between Canada and the United States, the river becomes the western boundary of Glacier National Park. The USDA states "river users find the views breathtaking and water clear and cold." I can attest to the accuracy of that statement. When the trout weren't biting, Shaya and I would frequently turn to look at the spectacular views of Glacier's mountains behind us.

Secondly, compared to most of the trout streams in the West, the North Fork remains lightly fished—especially north of Polebridge and inside GNP where we have been fortunate to enjoy so many wonderful hours wade fishing. Even now, it is unusual to see another person wade fishing there—though I know that could change at any time. We usually do see a few rafts floating down the river while we are fishing. Sometimes the rafts contain sightseers and sometimes fly fishers. Over the years, I have gone on many guided fly-fishing float trips down the North Fork and the same is true—you may see three or four other watercraft along the way.

Third, I discovered that the North Fork does indeed have a very healthy trout population. True, the Flathead River system can't compare with places like the Henry's Fork, the Madison, or the Missouri if you are counting trout by the square mile, because there's not as much food in the water. Also, the fish tend to be smaller. However, the relative lack of food has an advantage: The fish are hungry. They have only the summer months to pack on some weight. So, unlike the trout of the Henry's Fork, who turn up their noses at everything but the most delicately presented fly, the North Fork's trout are more opportunistic. If something is floating over-head that looks like dinner, they are inclined to take a swipe at it. Although there were many occasions where we did have to try to match the hatch on the Flathead, mostly we simply tied on one of our favorite flies and floated it down the river.

Finally, although the spots we have wade fished over the years were a good hour-long drive from our "lodge," they were relatively easy to get to by Montana standards. Somewhere along the line, I learned that the GNP rangers maintained a map of fishing access sites located inside the park north of Polebridge on the inside North Fork Road which heads to Kintla Lake. Within a relatively short period of time we had explored all the spots and had narrowed it down to the two that were the best. Then it was simply a matter of driving to the West entrance of GNP, cutting across the park on the Camas Road until it intersected with the outside North Fork Road, which we took for about twenty-five miles to Polebridge where we reentered the park and then drove for several miles on the inside North Fork Road until we came to the fishing spots. (Okay, so isn't that easy.) After reaching the first spot, we walked about one hundred yards to the river. There were several nice runs upstream that were very productive. The number of trout that we could catch when the fish were hungry is this spot was impressive. Most were in the eight to twelve inch range but sometimes we would hook one that was fifteen inches are more. And we caught them almost always on dry flies.

The second access spot is my all-time favorite place for wade fishing. It is located a few miles more up the road. A narrow channel about fifty feet wide separates an island from the main stem of the North Fork. After pulling off the road and getting ready to fish, we would wade across the channel to the island and bushwhack along it upstream for a few hundred yards before getting back into the river. On these trips we never forgot to bring our bear spray since this is prime grizzly habitat. I also made it a practice to sing Western cowboy songs as loudly as I could (such as "I Ride an Old Paint") so that the bears would know that there were humans in the area. This has proved to be a very effective deterrent. My singing is so gosh darned awful that bears within a range of five miles have been known to flee the area as fast as they can run. Although we have seen many grizzlies in Glacier National Park, we have never saw one while fishing the North Fork. Some people, though, warned us on one occasion that they had seen a griz about one hundred yards upstream just as we were about to get in the water.

Once we were back in the water, there were several runs along the inside of the island that sometimes held good fish. On one memorable day, we arrived in time for an actual hatch of tiny flies—perhaps pale morning duns or trico spinners. We don't carry many small dry flies because we usually don't need them, but fortunately after madly searching through my fly box I found a few flies that might do the trick. Shaya tied one on, tossed into the pool and hooked a big cutthroat almost immediately. She caught several nice trout in that run in the fifteen-inch or more category before the hatch ended. The next stop along the way is a hole we called the "trout nursery." This is a deep pool located in the channel at the very northern tip of the island. We could always count on catching trout there, but for some reason only the small fry. We never caught one larger than eight inches.

The best spot is a large pool perhaps a few hundred feet long located just north of the island. This is not easy wade fishing, though. When we reached this point, we entered the main stem of the North Fork. The rocks are slippery, and the current is tough—especially early in the year. Perhaps this why it is one place where I could usually out-fish my wife. Since I am taller, I could negotiate my way farther upstream than she. Like all trout fishing expeditions, there were days when the fishing was poor. But more often than not, it was excellent. It's astonishing how many trout were in this pool. Within the space of less than two hours, we frequently caught more than a couple of dozen between us. And they were not all little fish. We often brought to net beautiful cuts in the fifteen-inch range. When the fish were really hungry, it was not uncommon for two of them to attack a fly simultaneously coming from different directions. I am surprised that they did not bump heads and knock each other out.

Once we had finished fishing the pool, it was time to move down the western side of the island back towards where we had started. This stretch of the North Fork is bigger water—about fifty yards wide. I caught one of the biggest cutthroat of my life about two-thirds of the way down the island in a small pool during our first year of wade fishing the North Fork. I don't remember what fly I was using. What I do remember is the monster sucked in my dry fly and took off down the river in the fast current. I was convinced it was a bull trout but after playing the fish for ten minutes or so, I finally landed what turned out to be a cutthroat that easily weighed four pounds. Regretfully, I don't have a picture of it. I may have had a

The North Fork of the Flathead River—best wade fishing spot. AUTHOR'S COLLECTION.

camera with me but, if I did, I wanted to get the fish back in the water as quickly as possible. I don't remember where Shaya was, but she was not close enough to snap a photo with her camera.

Although wader fishing is my preferred method of fishing the North Fork, I have enjoyed many wonderful trips on the river fishing with a guide from a drift boat. Our ace guide is Cameron Houston. Shaya and I first met Cam on one of our early guided trips on the North Fork. The day we met Cam we had two guides because our friends from our Champaign-Urbana years, Bob and Bobbie Rosenthal, had come to visit us shortly after we purchased the lodge. So, Bob and I (the two "expert" fly fishers) went with one guide, while Shaya and Bobbie went with the other. As out turned out, Bob and I fished with Kurt, who is also a terrific guide; Shaya and Bobbie fished with Cam. Not long after the two boats started down the river, Cam asked Shaya where we lived. Shaya replied, "In Lynnewood Estates, just outside of Columbia Falls." Cam was surprised because his in-laws, Scott and Arlis, live across the street from us. They are good friends of ours. Bobbie, who was just learning to fly fish, caught one of the biggest mountain whitefish that we have seen come out of the North Fork. We all did pretty well that day, though Bob and I set a record on the North Fork for getting our lines tangled while fishing from a drift boat. Bob and Bobbie had just moved from the East Coast to Washington. Bob's "home" river had become the Yakima, a blue-ribbon river about two hours east of Washington. Our plan was that I would visit Bob so that the two of could fish the Yakima. But it never was to happen. A short while later, Bob passed away in his vehicle while returning from a fly-fishing trip. Bobbie was kind enough to send me several flies that Bob had hand tied. They are part of a memorial to Bob that hangs on the wall in our lodge.

But back to the action. Why trout bite better on some days than others on the North Fork is a mystery that defies explanation. I have learned some things, though. In general, the trout that inhabit the North Fork do not like changes in the weather. A few rain showers during a float trip can pretty much guarantee that you will have a mediocre day at best. Surprisingly, bright sunlight does not seem to bother them at all. In fact, they seem to prefer it. The time of day is important. The North Fork trout like to bite in the morning and again in the afternoon. Midday is tough. This, of course, is pretty much true of all freshwater game fish. Cam fishes the main stem of the Flathead with clients most days during the summer and the North Fork every so often. What I have learned from talking to him is that the fish can bite like crazy one day and the very next day develop a serious case of lockjaw for no apparent reason.

I was lucky enough on one of our float down the North Fork with Cam to have a day where the trout were ravenously hungry. Perhaps this was because hatches were actually happening—a rarity on this river. I started catching trout almost immediately after the put in. The thing about the North Fork is that it's loaded with small trout. And if the bigger ones aren't hungry, they may be all you catch. But I was catching some decent fish. About three hours into the trip, we stopped for lunch on a sandbar. But we noticed that fish were jumping all around us. I aid to Cam "to hell with lunch" and we got back in the drift boat. I made a few casts and hooked a monster. With Cam directing the action, I was able to land the fish. It was about twenty-one inches long and easily weighed four pounds—maybe more. Alas, as I held up the beauty so Cam could take a picture, it jumped out of my hands and back into the river. Cam said that it was the biggest cutthroat that he had ever seen come out of the North Fork. So, I guess I hold a kind of unofficial record, though I have not asked him lately if anyone he has guided has subsequently caught a bigger one. A short while later, I landed another big one. I do have a picture of this one, though it's much smaller than the monster that "got away."

Me with a big Northfork cutthroat trout. AUTHOR'S COLLECTION.

Wade Fishing Versus Drift Boat Fishing

This may be an appropriate time to make a comment about wade fishing versus drift boat fishing. As I mentioned earlier, although I have had the good fortune to make wonderful trips down the North Fork with excellent guides, to me there's no comparison. The term "Zen" I know is overused. But I can't think of a better word to describe how I feel when wade fishing. Wade fishing the North Fork for me is much like fishing Barton Creek. I become totally immersed in the moment. There's a sense of immediacy about the experience: It's just my fly rod, the water, the fish and me. And perhaps most importantly, I am making all the decisions: What section of a river to fish, what fly to use and where to toss my fly. Drift boat fishing is a different story. The guide generally is shouting directions such as "cast over by the rock, "Mend your line," etc. After about an hour in a drift boat, I start to become numb. Of course, it does have its advantages. You can cover many miles of a river, which increases your chances of encountering feeding fish. It also gives you a better shot on the North Fork of hooking a really big trout. And a trip down the North Fork is always a thing of beauty—even if the fish aren't cooperating. Of course, it's a different story if you own your own drift boat, but I never did. All in all, wade fishing is the kind of angling that I enjoy the most—by a long shot. Sadly, as Shaya and I are now in our mid-seventies, our wade-fishing days on the North Fork are drawing to a close.

A Word of Advice if You are Thinking about Taking Up Fly Fishing

Over the years, I wish had a dollar for every non-fly fisherperson who said to me, "I would like to try fly fishing, but it looks so difficult." My reply to them is always basically the same. I tell them not to be fooled by the mystique of fly fishing: It's not as daunting as it may look. To be sure, if you wish to become truly a master fly fisher, you will need to spend countless hours of studying aquatic biology and improving yours skills. But to become a competent fly fisher is not all that hard. On a day on the North Fork when the trout are actively feeding, I know from experience that with a little coaching a beginning fly fisher will soon have trout rising to his or her fly. In fact, Cam, Shaya and I took my oldest granddaughter, Emily, who was about ten at the time, out one evening on the North Fork so that she could practice fly casting. Since she has grown up in New Jersey, her fishing has been largely limited to a few ponds in the area. She took one look at the North Fork, which is so unlike any fishery she had ever seen before, and said, "Do fish actually live in here?" After ten minutes or so of instructions from Cam, she had several small cuts trying to eat her fly. Catching them, though takes a little more practice. If you are thinking about taking up fly fishing, take a casting lesson at your local fly shop, watch some videos on the Internet, invest some money in decent (but not overly expensive) equipment and get out on the water. If you have some extra money to spend, going out with a guide on the river for a half or full day is a great way to improve your skills.

Let me jump ahead in the story here to prove this point. Our good friends in Montana, Michael and Susan, purchased fly-fishing equipment several years ago. They even took a fly-fishing lesson. But their fly-fishing equipment remained unused—it was still in the box. They were too busy with their new house, traveling, and visiting with friends and family to get out on the water. A few years ago, I mentioned to Michael that Shaya and I were going to up to one of our favorite mountain lakes to fly fish. Michael allowed that he and Susan would like to join us. I said to Michael, "We would love to have you along on the expedition but there is one condition. You have to take your fly rods out of their boxes and use them when we get to the lake." Michael readily agreed and a few days later we headed up to the lake. When we arrived, however, Michael and Susan got cold feet. Michael said that they felt more comfortable using their spinning gear. So, they took their rods and reels out of their truck, put their kayaks in the water, and began fishing.

Shaya and I followed a few minutes later with our fly rods. Now, we have fished this lake many times and if the fish are biting, the action can be pretty fast. Shaya began catching one fish after another. We could see Michael and Susan from where we were fishing, and they were not having much luck with their spinning lures. So, after about a half an hour, we paddled over to them and asked if they would like to try their fly-fishing gear. They said, "Sure," so we paddled back to shore, where Shaya gave them a quick refresher course on casting and handed them each a few renegades. We all then paddled back out on the lake. For the next few hours, I could hear Michael whooping and hollering across the lake each time he hooked another fish. I think he caught at least a dozen fish and Susan caught quite a few as well. The moral of the story: Under certain conditions, fly fishing can more productive than spin fishing (or even fishing with live bait). The problem for most people is making the transition from equipment they feel comfortable using to using equipment that is unfamiliar to them. It just takes some time and patience to make the change.

Tips for Beginning Fly Fishers

I would be remiss if I did not offer at least some fly-fishing advice in this book. This advice is intended for beginners since I am certainly not in a position to offer advice to advanced anglers. Here goes:

1. The best way to begin is by taking a lesson from a competent fly-fishing instructor. This may be accomplished in two ways:

    (i) By taking a lesson at a local shop (some of them have pools where you can practice casting). Follow up on the lesson by practicing in your back yard or at a local stream or lake;

    (ii) By hiring a competent guide and taking a lesson out on the water. This can be frustrating at first, but you will learn a lot and may catch some fish. Again, follow up with practice at home.

Watching experts casting on videos is also a good way to improve your technique.

2. Like most things in life, experience is the best teacher. I have certainly learned a good deal from other fly fishers over the years, but most of what I know I learned on my own. What makes fly fishing fascinating is that trout and their related species, in particular, are fickle. So, the fly that worked just great yesterday may not catch a thing today. Learning to change flies every ten to fifteen minutes is important. You will have favorite "go to" flies, though, that you use regularly. For me, an olive elk hair caddis has been one of my top producers in Montana, while Shaya does extremely well using a renegade. We both love to fish dry flies, but we have learned the hard way that casting a dry fly often will not produce any results if the fish are eating below the surface. Thus, we have learned to use wet flies. You will become more versatile as you gain experience. I do not often fish a more than one fly but tying a small wet fly to your large dry fly (a "dropper") can be effective.

3. When purchasing your first fly-fishing equipment, you don't need to break the bank. The fly rod is the most important item you will buy. A nine-foot., five-weight rod is a good way to start out for trout. You can purchase a terrific fly rod from companies like Orvis or TFO for about $150. I always read the guarantee carefully when buying a fly rod. Chances are you will break it at some point. Good companies guarantee their rods for ten years or more and will repair or replace for not much money. Your fly line is extremely important too: A quality line will run you about $50. Less important is the reel, unless you intend to go after big game fish. A perfectly suitable reel should run you no more than $75. Waders, boots, wading staffs, vests, nets and all the other accouterments that you need to fly fish probably will run you around $800. Okay, maybe that sounds expensive but most of this gear will last for years to come. Finally, you will need some flies: I would recommend starting out with a dozen dry flies and a dozen wet flies. I would not recommend buying the "assortments" that you find in big chain fishing stores. Have someone who is knowledgeable about what flies work in the area you will be fishing help you select them. BE ON THE LOOKOUT FOR SALES! You can save a bundle of money.

Red Meadow Lake: The Lake of the Mystery Fish

On our first tour of the West in the T@B, we began checking out places to fish in the environs of the tourist town of Whitefish—something we had not done before. Luckily, at Bad Rock Books in downtown Columbia Falls, I found a wonderful older book on fishing western Montana's rivers and lakes published over forty years ago. It is beautifully written and some of the information in it is still accurate. Red Meadow Lake was one of the bodies of water mentioned in the book that I found intriguing. It's a small lake—sixteen acres—located about twenty-five miles up a logging road about a half an hour west of Whitefish at an elevation of over five thousand feet. So, one day Shaya and I took off in the Highlander to see if we could find the lake. After the usual wrong turns, we arrived at Red Meadow about ten o'clock in the morning. We saw fish jumping—always a good sign for fly fishers. This was before we had our inflatable kayak, so I donned my waders while Shaya said she would fish from shore. Red Meadow is a fairly shallow lake with a maximum depth of about eleven feet. (The lake may have been deeper before a famous avalanche hit it years ago, sending rocks crashing into the water and, according to local legend, fish flying into the surrounding forest.)

I began working my way around the lake to the right, casting into deeper water. We both started catching silver colored fish in the six to nine inch range on a variety of dry flies. These were definitely not the cutthroats that I remembered my forty-year old guidebook said inhabited Red Meadow Lake. Nor were they rainbow trout. I decided to hike around to the backside of the lake where I found a submerged rock ledge that extended out into the water. The hungry silvery fish were all around me. They came rocketing out of the depths to take a whack at my royal coachman like they had been shot out of a submarine. But for every fish I caught four or five got away—they had tiny mouths. After catching about twenty or more, it was time to head back to where Shaya was fishing from shore.

I was puzzled by these mystery fish. My best guess is that they were mountain whitefish, though I could not imagine how so many could have come to live in the lake. She was puzzled by the fish too. She said to me, "These fish have a really big dorsal fin," stretching out the fin on one that she had just caught a minute before releasing it back into the lake. A light bulb went on in my head. I said to her, "Where's the guide book? I am sure I brought it with us. I think it has pictures of trout in it." Sure enough, it did—beautiful color plates. And when I looked up "arctic grayling" my suspicions were confirmed. I saw that it included the arctic grayling right below cutthroat trout. I was embarrassed that I had not immediately known what the fish were, but then again I had only caught one arctic grayling in my whole life and that was many years before on a guided trip in Idaho. Red Meadow is, in fact, the lake that we had taken Michael and Susan to try their luck with fly rods.

On our first journey to the West in the T@B, I kept a journal of our fishing expeditions. After returning from Red Meadow, I wrote in the journal, "What a treat! I hope to return to Red Meadow many times more to fish for those 'mountain whitefish' before hanging up my fly rod." I am happy to say that we have indeed fished Red Meadow at least a dozen times over the years.

The Montana Field Guide states that the Montana Arctic grayling "has a large, sail-like dorsal fin and colorful body markings." Their dorsal fins are "typically fringed in red and dotted with large iridescent red, aqua, or purple spots and markings." The only populations of this fish in the Lower 48 states were found in Montana and Michigan. The Michigan population is now extinct and in Montana it is extremely endangered. The last river dwelling remnants of the grayling in Montana are found in the Big Hole River. Lewis and Clark made note of these "new kind of white or silvery fish trout in 1805."

I don't remember exactly when it was that we met John Moore at Red Meadow. I do know that it was many years ago. When we arrived at the lake on one of our expeditions, we parked next to a truck with a camper on the back of it. We also noticed a fisherperson in a rowboat working the middle of the lake. He looked like he knew what he was doing. We grabbed our fly rods, launched the inflatable kayak and paddled down the right side of the lake. By this time, we had our modus operandi down pat on Red Meadow. We like to work the far shoreline with our fly rods, looking for rising grayling. Shaya is always in the front of the kayak and thus has first shot at the fish. This is my excuse for why she almost always out fishes me on Red Meadow—I am too busy "guiding." The fish were actively feeding that day, so we were catching an assortment of grayling in the six to twelve inch category. After a few hours, we decided to call it a day. The fishing drops off on Red Meadow around noon; and, if you want to have some action again, you need to wait until the late afternoon when the sun begins to go down behind the mountains. We paddled back to shore to put our gear away and had lunch. A few minutes after we landed, the gentleman in the boat rowed back to shore. Now, I like to talk to other fishermen, so we introduced ourselves. He introduced himself as John Moore. John mentioned that he liked to camp at Red Meadow in the small parking lot so that he could fish the lake in the morning and the evening.

It turned out that John Moore is not just another fisherperson. He, in fact, has held ten certified Washington state records, though some of them have been surpassed by now. He's also an author of *A Fisherman's Guide to Selected Lakes of Northwest Montana* in three volumes published in 2007, 2010, and 2015. Moore's books are somewhat unusual in that they rarely give detailed descriptions of how to catch the fish in the hundreds of lakes he has visited. Instead, he provides a detailed description of how to get to each lake, a description of the lake itself and a summary of what species of fish he has caught in the lake (if any). Many of the lakes he did not bother to fish because of a time factor or because they are simply too big for his boat. A typical entry for a lake where he has had success might be, "Flies fished from shore are very effective." So, he tends to disappoint readers who would prefer much more information on how to fish a particular body of water.

The truly astounding thing about John is that he has actually made it to the hundreds of lakes catalogued in his books. If you are at all familiar with northwest Montana, you know how rugged this country is. Many of the lakes he has journeyed to require a long drive down boulder strewn logging roads followed by arduous hikes of many miles up into the mountains. And he's never been lost. John was unabashedly selling his book from the back of his truck. Naturally, we purchased one, which he autographed, and he threw in one of his favorite flies as a bonus. Today, I own all three volumes. They are fun to scan at night when I am searching for another lake to try. How good of a fisherperson is John? Well, let's just say he's caught over two hundred grayling in a single day at Red Meadow. Over the years, we have had the good fortune on several occasions to fish Red Meadow at the same time as John. It's one of his favorite lakes. It's one of ours, too.

Moose Lake: The Lake of No Refusals

On one of our early excursions to the North Fork, we were camped in the T@B at the Big Creek campground several miles south of Polebridge. The fishing was bad, which is why I found myself whining to the campground hostess one morning that were not having any luck. Over the years, I have discovered that whining to a person who may know something about the local fishing is a good practice: The person may take pity on you and provide you with some invaluable information. In this case, it worked. She said to me, "Why don't you try Moose Lake?" My response, of course, was predictable. I said, "Moose Lake? Where's that?" She explained that it was in the mountains about twenty-five miles up the Coal Creek Road and that fishing was good for pan-sized cutthroat trout. So, after she gave me directions, Shaya and I took off in the Highlander to find the lake.

I remember that day well. It was miserable—raining and cold. When we arrived a few hours later, we parked the Highlander in the small parking lot and walked about one hundred yards down a path to the lake. A nice young man was standing on the shore fishing with his son. We started talking. He mentioned that he was from Canada and also told me that they had not much luck. But with the weather as bad as it was, I was not surprised. I took a long look at Moose Lake and decided it was worth another trip when the weather cleared.

A few days later we returned. This was again before I had purchased the inflatable kayak, so we donned our waders, strung up our fly rods and headed down the path. Moose Lake, like Red Meadow, is small. The Montana Department of Fish, Wildlife & Parks describes it as about twenty acres in size with a maximum depth of fourteen and a half feet. The water in this lake is extremely clear. The western side of the lake has a long shelf that runs out to a drop off located perhaps one hundred feet from shore. So, you can walk down to the lake and begin wade fishing. The only problem is that you tend to sink down into the muck as you walk farther out into the lake—not fun. I waded out and began casting towards rising fish. I caught one and then another and another. The incredible thing about fishing Moose Lake is that the water is so clear that you can see the trout beneath the surface chasing your dry fly. The campground hostess was right about the size of the cutthroat trout: They are small. In all my years of fishing Moose Lake, I have never caught one that was more than twelve inches long. What the campground hostess failed to mention was that the cutthroat trout of Moose Lake are the most beautiful that I have ever seen. The colors on these fish are so brilliant that there's only one word to describe them: gaudy. They appear to have been colored with Day Glo paint. Why this is, I don't know. Perhaps it is what they eat.

For the first few years that we fished Moose Lake, I did not yet have the kayak, so we were wade fishing from shore. The action was usually fast; but once we had the kayak, it improved exponentially. Now we had the whole lake at our disposal. Over the years, the far shore has actually proved to be more productive. The *modus operandi* for fishing Moose

Gaudy Westslope Cutthroat Trout, Moose Lake. AUTHOR'S COLLECTION.

Lake is much like that for Red Meadow. We look for rising fish and paddle over to them. The astounding thing about Moose is how many fish you can catch in three or four hours. Shaya, who almost always out fishes me on this lake (So what else is new?), has landed around ninety in a single day. The renegade, once again, has been our fly of choice in recent years; though a variety of dry flies would dry do the trick. A fishing pal once asked me about how often the cutthroats at Moose Lake refused to take a fly that had been proffered to them. My answer, which was only a bit of an exaggeration, was that at Moose Lake "There are no refusals." I often think it would be a great place to take a youngster to learn how to fly fish.

The Brook Trout of Swiftcurrent Lake:
The Legacy of the Eastern Elite

Over the years, we have made the hour-and-a-half drive from our "lodge" to the east side of Glacier National Park which is definitely more remote and perhaps even more spectacularly beautiful than West Glacier. There are three primary areas to explore: Two Medicine Lake, Saint Mary, and Many

Glacier. Thanks to Shaya, we discovered Aspenwood, a delightful combination RV campground and bed-and-breakfast located on the Blackfeet Indian Reservation about nine miles from Browning. Using Aspenwood as our base camp, we could would take many wonderful hikes over the years and also try our luck fishing in the eastern side of GNP.

The beautiful and historic Many Glacier Hotel is located, not surprisingly, in the Many Glacier area of GNP. The hotel overlooks Swiftcurrent Lake, which some of the young hotel employees informed me has a robust population of eastern brook trout. This species is not native to Montana. Its natural range in the United States is limited to the eastern states as far west as Minnesota (where Shaya and I fished for them with brother Joe in our younger days). So how did the eastern brook trout find its way to Montana? The answer lies in the early history of the blue-blood conservationists led by George Bird Grinnell who is considered the "Father" of Glacier National Park. In the early twentieth century, people like Grinnell wanted not only to preserve the nature that they found in the West—they very often wanted to improve on it. What better way to enhance the already splendid variety of sports fish found in Montana than to introduce the Eastern brook trout to its waters? So, Grinnell and his associates began stocking the brook trout in GNP's waters. Today, the great, great descendants many times over of those stocked trout survive in several of the park's lakes and rivers. The Park Service's attitude towards non-native fish introduced into Glacier's waters has changed one hundred and eighty degrees from the time of Grinnell. What we now know that Grinnell did not know then, as I previously discussed, is that non-native species stocked in lakes and streams often have disastrous consequences for the native species. This is why Park Service has a healthy daily limit allowed on keeping brook trout.

For some reason, I was at first reluctant to take the inflatable kayak out on Swiftcurrent. The lake looked sort of foreboding to me. And it is true that because of where it is located, storms can blow up on it in an instant. My fears, of course, were grossly overblown, having more to do with my often ridiculously high anxiety level that with any real danger. In the end, my desire to try our luck catching brook trout overrode my anxiety level.

So, many years ago, with fly rods in hand we launched the kayak from the access spot on the northern side of the lake. Swiftcurrent is not a large lake compared to many of the giants in GNP like St. Mary and Kintla. It is only about one hundred acres and is relatively shallow. I would be remiss if I did not mention that it is an incredibly beautiful lake with the glorious Mount Wilbur rising behind its western shore.

The brook trout fishing was phenomenal the first year we fished Swiftcurrent. We quickly discovered that the best fishing in the lake was around an area we called the "beach" about a twenty minute paddle to the right from there we launched the kayak. There's a series of points that run out into the lake from this area with sharp drop offs where the trout hang out. We could either fish from the kayak casting in towards shore or

Brook trout on the beach, Swiftcurrent Lake, Montana.
AUTHOR'S COLLECTION.

land the kayak on the beach and fish from shore. Either way was effective. I remember using royal coachmen that first year. The action was so fast that Shaya and I often had brook trout on the line at the same time. How big were they? The Swiftcurrent brookies are not huge. I think the biggest one we ever caught was maybe fifteen inches. But they fight like the devil.

After the first year, the fishing dropped off—much like it had on Barton Creek years before. Why is that the first year of fishing a body of water is often the best year for me? Is it just the luck of the draw or is something intangible going on? Have you had the same experience? I would have one more experience like this, which we will get to later. The fishing was still good, but we had to rely a lot more heavily on fishing wet flies. Both

Shaya and I much prefer to fish dry flies; however, I have done enough reading about fly fishing to know that trout feed a lot more on food they find below the surface than they do on food on the surface. In fact, one of our major evolutions as fly fishers was to begin fishing subsurface much more often than we had in our earlier years. So, when we could not coach the brookies to inhale dry flies, we tossed leech patterns into the depths. Why we started to use leech patterns I do not remember. Undoubtedly somebody who knew a lot more about fly fishing than we did suggested it. And the fact is that we often use leech patterns now not only for trout but also for smallmouth bass. The modus operandi at Swiftcurrent is to toss a leech fly into the depths and count to ten before starting to strip it in slowly. If the fish are hungry, a brookie will grab the leech and the fight is on. It is amazing how on different days different color leeches will work better than other colors. Sometimes the brookies prefer black; sometimes green; sometimes brown, etc. This is also true of the other spots where we fish leech patterns. On a good day, we might catch at least a dozen brookies or more using leech patterns. Because Swiftcurrent is home to the Many Glacier Hotel, it's better to fish the lake relatively early in the season. Later on, tourists tend to clutter up the lake, though very few of them are serious fisherpersons.

The other "obstacle" to fishing Swiftcurrent is the historic wooden boat, Chief Two Guns, which takes vacationers on scenic tours of the lake. Shaya is afraid of this boat because its path from the lodge to the dock at the far at the lake takes it right across where we fish from the kayak. On more than one occasion, Shaya has shouted at the captain for fear that the boat will run us over. And on more than one occasion, the captain has shouted back that we need to move because the lake is so shallow that they have to follow a narrow channel to keep Chief Two Guns from running aground. It's not really a problem, though. There's zero chance the boat would hit us. Last year, Shaya and I were fishing in the kayak off of one of our favorite points when Two Guns came steaming by. The boat was no more than thirty feet away from us when I hooked a big brook trout. After a short but furious battle, Shaya netted the fish. The admiring tourists on the boat applauded and gave "thumbs up" signs. That made my day. By the way, the boat tour is a lot of fun if you ever make it to Many Glacier.

Chief Two Guns *in front of the Many Glacier Lodge.* AUTHOR'S COLLECTION.

Shaya on the "Beach" at Swiftcurrent Lake, Glacier National Park. AUTHOR'S COLLECTION.

The "Culture" of Montana, Fishing the Mighty Missouri & the Night of the Deer (oh Dear!)

The second summer we owned the lodge, Mike, a good friend from our Champaign-Urbana days, came in early September to visit and do some fly fishing. This was before I had purchased the inflatable kayak, so we were limited to wade fishing or hiring a guide to float the rivers. Also, early September is not a propitious time to fish in northwestern Montana: The water temperature in the rivers is generally too high and the water levels too low. To be honest, I was feeling somewhat anxious about how we would do. We hiked into Stanton Lake on a miserably hot day for our neck of the woods, and there we caught a few small cuts. Then we made the long drive to Red Meadow, where had a fun day catching some grayling from shore. We fished the main stem of the Flathead from the Blankenship Bridge where we caught a few trout and some mountain whitefish. We hired Kurt to guide on the North Fork and the fishing was pretty good, except that I was tormented by horse flies that bit my ankles all the way down the river. Alas, we could not make it to Moose Lake because of road construction. I saved the BIG adventure for the last: A guided trip with Cam on the Missouri River.

I first learned about fly fishing on the Missouri years before from a father and son we met in Idaho who informed Shaya and me that they had caught so many big rainbows that their arms were tired the next day from pulling them in. But I had forgotten about the Missouri until I was reminded about the river by our veterinarian, Mark Lawson, who took care of our Old English Sheepdog. Mark was a high-powered vet in Atlanta before relocating to Columbia Falls in 2005. In addition to being a great veterinarian, he is also an expert fly fisher.

The thing about Montana is that hunting and fishing are really important to the inhabitants. And, since the pace of life is more relaxed than, say, in Atlanta, Chicago or New York, people take the time to discuss things—especially if has to do with the great out-of-doors. So, when I would take Sarie in to see Mark, which was quite frequent because of her advanced age, we would typically spend ten to fifteen minutes discussing fly fishing before he even looked at Sarie. I remember well the day Mark showed me photos of huge rainbows he had caught on the Missouri. That confirmed a story we had heard from father and son fly fishers. So, after Mark showed me the photographs, I made a mental note to try my luck on the Missouri someday.

And Mark was far from the only person I encountered who would spend a good chunk of time talking fly fishing before getting down to work. In addition to Mark, I can think of three others right of the bat. The first was Gary, our lawn maintenance person, who showed me photos of giant rainbows he had brought to net early in the spring when the ice first goes out. The second was our arborist, Brian, another expert fly fisher with whom I spent many enjoyable minutes swapping fly fishing stories, and the third, Richard, with whom I discussed fishing for lunker brook trout for a good while before he cut down a couple of dead trees for us. So, before Mike came to visit, I explained to him that when you meet a person in Montana, it was customary first to discuss fly fishing before you talked about anything else, otherwise they might be offended. I was amazed by what happened after he arrived. Practically everybody we met asked us about fly fishing. Where we were fishing? What kind of flies were we using? And what were we catching? And, of course, they all wished us good luck. It was almost as if I had paid them in advance to make my words of wisdom come true. I am not a hunter, but I imagine the same thing is true for hunters in Montana: Discussing what you are hunting for, where you are hunting and what you are bagging takes precedence over everything else.

Cam mainly guides on the stems of the Flathead River, but he also guides on the Blackfeet, the Clark Fork and Missouri, among others. So, I booked Cam to guide for Mike and me. It's about a 218-mile, four-hour drive, from Columbia Falls to Craig, Montana, a small town at the epicenter of fly fishing on the Missouri, which meant we would have to stay overnight. I booked a motel room for Mike and me, and we took off in the Highlander in the morning so that we would have time to do some wade fishing before fishing with Cam the next day. We arrived in time to wet our lines but did not have any luck. We met Cam early the following morning at the access site and within a half on hour were on the water.

The best trout fishing on the Missouri is found on a stretch of the river from the Holter Dam to the city of Cascade, thirty-five miles downriver. This stretch of the Missouri averages some 5,500 trout per square mile and many of the rainbows and browns exceed twenty inches. As I was to discover, the tailrace right below the dam is the most popular place to fish. By around 9 am, at least twenty drift boats were parading in a circle below the dam. The best way that I can describe fishing the tailrace is to compare it to being on a merry-go-round. People come from all over the United States and also foreign countries to fish this water, so the crowd should not have surprised me. This stretch of the Missouri gets weedy in the later summer and early fall. Cam had Mike and me fishing small wet flies. The problem with fishing wet flies in the weeds is that when something tugs on your line, you don't know if it is a fish or a weed. But just in case it is a fish, you have to set the hook. This means you are setting your hook every few minutes. Alas, on the day we were fishing, ninety-nine percent of the time it was a weed.

We did land some nice sized rainbows, though. As the guest, we put Mike in the front of the boat. He caught some nice fish but also lost one or two due to his inexperience. Now Cam is a pretty low-key guide who does not scream and yell at his clients like a lot of guides. But I remember one instance in which Mike had hooked a big rainbow and for some reason wound up with about thirty or forty feet of loose fly line around him and in the water. I remember Cam saying something like "Mike, I know you can do better than that." The fish got away. We had only booked Cam for one day. In retrospect, I should have booked him for two days. He had another client booked for the following day and later reported to me that this fisherperson had a much better day than we. Cam's explanation for this is that because he had not fished the Missouri in some time, it took him most of the first day to figure out what the fish were eating; by the second day, he had solved the problem. To his credit, Cam still apologizes to me for this. But, you know what? I am still happy we fished with him because hiring a guide you do not know can be a real crapshoot.

The big adventure on this trip, though, was yet to come. We were off the water by around 4 pm and instead of staying in Craig overnight, we headed for home. This turned out to be a terrible mistake. Most of the drive between Columbia Falls and Craig is on Highway 83 through the Swan Valley. This is real wilderness. On one side of the road is the Swan Mountain range; on the other side is the Mission Mountain range. Driving from Columbia Falls to Craig was not a problem because we left in the morning; driving from Craig to Columbia Falls starting in the late afternoon proved to be another kettle of fish altogether. The problem was that in September in Montana it begins to get dark by around 5 pm. So, we were losing daylight just as we hit Highway 83. The other problem— and a far worse one—is that a thick fog began to settle in. Why we did not make the decision to just pull the Highlander over by the side of the road and sleep in it overnight, I do not know. We had cell phones with us, but I don't remember if we had service in that remote area. I think that we may have been worried that Shaya would be worried about us if we were not home by around 9 pm. In any case, I slowed down to about 20 MPH, but it was not enough.

All of a sudden, a deer appeared out of gloom on the road directly in front of us. I slammed on the brakes but to no avail. I hit the deer head on. We stopped the car to inspect the damage to the front of the Highlander. It was bad, but the vehicle was not out of commission. I do not know what happened to the deer. It disappeared into the woods. I don't know what we would have done had we found it. Neither of us had a firearm with which to humanely dispatch the deer and there was no one around to administer first aid to a badly wounded animal. We got back into the Highlander. For some reason, I had not learned my lesson. We decided to press on. I slowed down even more but there were deer all around us. About twenty minutes later, I hit a second deer. This time the Highlander sustained even more damage.

I was seriously rattled. Mike saved the day by using a fish stringer he happened to have with him to tie the Highlander's bumper to the front of the vehicle. At that point, he took over driving. Fortunately, the fog began to lift. But within about twenty miles of Columbia Falls, a big buck jumped out from the side of the highway and bounced off the side of the Highlander. It ran back into the fields. We finally arrived back at the lodge around 11 pm.

Shaya was happy to see us. The Highlander, it turned out, had sustained about $5,000 in damages. Much to my dismay, Mike and I may hold the unofficial state of Montana record for clocking deer in one day.

The moral of the story is that one should never embark on an extended drive through a remote wilderness area at night, especially when it's foggy. In defense of myself, this happened the second summer we were in Montana. I did not know any better. Since then, I have heard many stories about what highways to avoid at night. For example, the drive between Whitefish and Eureka is famous for being dangerous. And I have subsequently heard lots of stories about the drive down the Swan Valley on Highway 83. Cam himself hit a deer several years ago driving home at night from the Missouri. Now when I drive after sunset in Montana even around Columbia Falls, I rarely exceed fifty miles per hour. I don't care how many people honk at me. In fact, according to an article by Brett French in the September 20, 2016, edition of the *Billings Gazette,* Montana ranks second only to West Virginia per capita in the number of vehicle-versus-large wildlife collisions.

The Montanans' Love Affair with the Huckleberry

We have already established that Montanans love to hunt and fish. And they also enjoy eating the game that they have hunted and the fish they have caught. But there's arguably one thing they enjoy consuming more than even venison or rainbow trout, and that is the huckleberry. Now, if you do not hail from Montana or have never visited Big Sky country, your only familiarity with the word "huckleberry" may be from watching the hit TV animated cartoon program, *The Huckleberry Hound Show,* which ran from 1958 to 1961. You may remember that he was an affable, blue-skinned canine with a Southern drawl. Huckleberry's name was a reference to the Mark Twain novel, *The Adventures of Huckleberry Finn.* It turns out that there are four species of huckleberries found in North America. The red huckleberry is the one prized by Montanans. Since attempts to cultivate huckleberry plants have met with abject failure, you must drive off into the wilds in order to get some. This is not such an easy task. First, you have to find huckleberry bushes by driving up and down remote gravel roads in the mountains. Once you locate a patch, you must strap a pail onto your body and carefully pick your way through trees and branches until you reach the berries. If you are lucky, the patch you have discovered has not been picked over so that you can quickly fill your pail to the brim. Then, it's time to head back to your vehicle with your precious cargo. Oh, I forgot, there's more obstacle to picking huckleberries: Grizzly bears. Grizzlies love huckleberries, too. So, you must always be "bear aware" when picking them. Several years ago, a grizzly bear chased a teenage boy huckleberry picker for a mile and a half, all the way around a local lake. He narrowly escaped with his berries and his life.

I can always tell the local Montanans from the transplants when I am picking huckleberries: The locals carry gigantic pistols on their hips, while the transplants have bear spray. The demand for huckleberries is so great that locals often supplement their income by selling berries that they have picked. Wholesale they normally go for around $20 per pound. But if you wished to buy a pound of "hucks" off the Internet today, you might pay up to $50 per pound!

What do locals do with the huckleberry? Although "hucks" are not very tasty right off the bush, they are wonderful when made into pies or ice cream. And pies and ice cream are just the beginning. If you should ever make it to Hungry Horse, Montana, located a few miles south of Glacier National Park, you must stop by the Huckleberry Patch. My guess is that the Huckleberry Patch has more than a hundred products made out of "hucks" on its shelves. Don't leave without trying a scoop of their huckleberry ice cream!

We Meet a Legendary Park Ranger.

Bowman and Kintla are the two most remote lakes that you can drive to in GNP. Both are located on the Inside North Fork Road above Polebridge. In order to access them, you drive up the North Fork Road to Polebridge and then enter the park at the Polebridge Ranger Station. To get to Bowman, you turn off on to a long and bumpy road a few miles after the station.

Now, this spectacularly beautiful lake of more than 1,700 acres is not noted for its excellent fishing. But one day when the weather forecast looked especially propitious for a kayaking trip to the lake (little wind), we decided to take our fly-fishing gear with us. Our plan was to paddle down the long narrow lake as far as we dared and then turn around. If for some reason, it looked like we might have a chance to catch a fish or two, we would make some casts. After arriving, we tossed the Saturn in the lake and headed down the right shore. If you are a fisherperson the thing you would notice right away about Bowman is how barren the rock strewn bottom of the lake looks: There is simply is not a lot of plant life. This means that there's not a lot of critters in the water for the fish to eat. Hence, the fish population is not abundant. But make no mistake about it; it does hold some fish, as we were about to find out.

To our surprise, about thirty minutes into the excursion, we saw some fishing jumping ahead of us. Shaya tied on a Parachute Madam X as I paddled towards them. Now, I have not mentioned this fly so far, but it's a good one. I am not sure why we had them in our fly box at the time—it may have been Bob Arens, the master flyer tier in Columbia Falls recommended the Madam X to us. According to information on the Internet, it is a creation of Doug Swisher and is fished as an imitation for everything from hoppers to stoneflies and some terrestrials. I don't remember what color she was using—might have been red, orange or chartreuse. On her third or fourth cast, a big fish came up out of the depths and inhaled the fly. After a brief but exciting battle, I netted it. It was a cutthroat trout that easily went three pounds and maybe was closer to four! We were both astounded. A few minutes later, I caught one that was easily as big as Shaya's. We landed a few more cuts before the action ended. It was one of those days where we just happened to be in the right place at the right time. Our return trips to Bowman have not been productive, but still it's a beautiful lake to kayak.

The ride to Kintla Lake takes even longer than the one to Bowman. Instead of the turning off the Inside North Fork Road as we do to get to Bowman, we keep going straight for more than twenty miles. It's only slightly smaller than Bowman and, if anything, is even more beautiful.

Kintla—like Bowman—is not a great fishing lake. Most of our trips to the lake have just been for recreational kayaking. However, years ago our friend Sandy (you may remember her from our fishing experience on the Wolf River earlier in this journal) came to visit us in Montana with her second husband, Gabe. This was in August 2010—one year before we had purchased the lodge—so we were all staying in a rustic cabin at the wonderful Abbott Valley Homestead outside of Martin City. Shaya and I decided that we would take the two of them on a sightseeing trip to Kintla. I would also give Sandy a fly-fishing lesson after we reached the lake. We did not as yet own any kayaks, so the plan was that Sandy would borrow Shaya's waders and fly-fishing outfit, while Shaya and Gabe watched from shore. Kintla does have a decent population of small cutthroats that like to hang out by the creek where it runs into the lake.

When we arrived, I could see some small fishing jumping fifty feet or so out in the lake. So, Sandy and I waded out from shore. While I began instructing Sandy on the intricacies of fly fishing, Shaya and Gabe walked down the path along the shoreline that leads to a little bridge that crosses Kintla Creek. Of course, she had her fly rod in hand. By now you should be able to guess what happened next. When they reached the bridge, Shaya began to make some casts into the creek. Within a few seconds, she had hooked a feisty cutthroat and then another one and another one. Here I was, the master fly fisher, floundering around in the lake without so much as catching a single trout, while Shaya was pulling them one in after another from the bridge. Now, when Shaya hooks a fish, she invariably says, "Got one," which I actually much prefer to the somewhat pretentious, "Fish on," which seems to me appropriate only if you have just hooked something really big like a marlin or sailfish out in the deep blue sea. About the sixth time she hollered, "Got one," I had had enough. Sandy and I waded back to the shore took off our waders and headed down to the bridge. It's been many years since this expedition, so I am no longer remember whether Sandy or I caught any trout from the bridge.

But the big highlight of this trip was not catching some trout. It was meeting the legendary—and I mean, legendary—Park Ranger Lyle Ruterbories.

If you do not think that Lyle is actually a legend, I invite you to type in "Lyle Ruterbories Kintla Lake Ranger" on your search engine. Several stories about him will pop up. He began his career as a seasonal park ranger in 1993 at the age of 73. Before that he was a volunteer campground host at Kintla with his wife, Mary, who passed away in 2005. A 2013 National Park Service article, "Kintla Lake Park Ranger Ponders Retirement," states:

> Ruterbories often goes above and beyond his daily duties, contributing countless hours to numerous projects. He has built log barrier structures for each campsite parking spot to protect vegetation, constructed a log rail fence around Kintla Ranger Station complex, leveled all Kintla campsites, and constructed walking paths to Kintla Creek and the beach area of Kintla Lake. Ruterbories refinished the wood floor of the Kintla Ranger Station himself and still pulls weeds in the Kintla Lake campground on almost daily."

While Shaya, Sandy and I were busy fishing; Gabe had a chance to converse with Lyle. Gabe later wrote a poem about Lyle, which he gave to the old ranger who put it up in his cabin. The poem is reproduced here:

Gabe with park ranger Lyle Ruterbories.
AUTHOR'S COLLECTION.

Shaya with park ranger Lyle Ruterbories.
AUTHOR'S COLLECTION.

PARK RANGER
by Gabriel Heilig

You, sir—
Lyle Ruterbories,
ninety and still smiling,
voice firm and kind,
still able to reach in
and take out
from the lake
its rainbow trout.
You turn it over,
showing us where
its spots and shimmer
once got interbred
with the typical
trout cut
in its throat.

Ninety years,
you tell us—
and still at work,
taking out and
turning over
rainbows
from the waters
of the world.

The fact is that Ruterbories did not retire in 2013. The latest article I found about him on the Internet from a publication called "sages" is dated June 10, 2017. Ruterbories was still serving as a park ranger at the age of ninety-seven. That is probably about the time that Shaya and I last saw him at the Polebridge Ranger Station.

Fishing the Reservation with the
Legendary Blackfeet Guide, Joe Kipp

I do not remember exactly when we first learned about the rainbow trout fishing on the Blackfeet Reservation. It may very well have been from Bob Arens, who owns a fly-fishing shop in Columbia Falls. Bob, as I have mentioned, is a master fly tier. His shop is filled with just about every dry fly and wet fly that one could think of. He is also an expert fly fisherperson who has spent countless hours angling on the Blackfeet reservation. The sprawling reservation is one example where man's attempt to improve upon nature has succeeded. The reservation has more than two-dozen lakes but none of them contained trout until rainbows were stocked decades ago to provide food for the local population and boost the local economy by encouraging tourism. All in all, the plan has worked out splendidly. The Blackfeet have done an excellent job of managing the lakes. Some of the lakes contain huge rainbow trout. Duck Lake and Mission Lake, to name a few, have been famous over the years for producing whopper trout in the ten- to fifteen-pound range.

There are a few problems, though, with fishing the Blackfeet reservation for outsiders. First, is finding the lake you hope to fish. The map that the Blackfeet Fish and Wildlife Department provides for fisherpersons does not give detailed directions to the lakes. Signs directing you to a lake for the most part do not exist. And even a GPS is of limited use. The Blackfeet people are more than willing to help you out, but their directions can be hard to follow. For example, they might tell you that to find a lake you need to drive about ten miles south of Browning on highway 89 until you cross Two Medicine Creek, then look for a pine tree about a mile down the road on the left hand side. When you pass the pine tree, take the first gravel road on the right. Drive for about two miles down the road until it forks. Take the right hand fork for another mile or so until you go over a big hill. Then take the next left and you will soon arrive at the lake. These directions are a pretty fair approximation of how we were told to get to Mitten Lake, the very first lake we fished on the rez. Mitten is a beautiful lake, but we fished way too late in the season. We did not catch any trout, but we did see some beautiful white pelicans. Of course, it's not a problem for the Blackfeet people to find the lake because they were living on the land for centuries even before it became a reservation in 1896. Then there's the problem of the wind. Much of the reservation consists of rolling plains. When the wind starts blowing, it can be ferocious. I am talking in the thirty- to fifty-mile-an-hour range. This means that there are lots of days when you simply can't fish.

Years ago, I started thinking about hiring a guide to fish the reservation. One name kept popping up in my conversations with people: Joe Kipp. Joe is a Blackfeet Tribal member who has been guiding fisherpersons and hunters on Blackfeet lands since 1985. In fact, I heard so much about Joe Kipp's exploits as a fishing guide that I began referring to him at some point as "the legendary Blackfeet fishing guide." I gave Joe a call one summer day many years ago and booked a trip with him. (By the way, he's so busy you had better call him at least a month in advance to arrange a trip.) Joe met us early one morning at the Sleeping Wolf Campground in Browning. Unfortunately, he did not have good news for us. The weather forecast was a front to blow in around 10 am with high winds. Joe told us that he had wanted to take us to Mission Lake where the fishing for big trout had been good recently, but it was too far away: By the time we got there, the storm front would have arrived, and we would be unable to fish it. So, we headed out to a nearby lake. Joe fishes from a large aluminum boat rigged up with a trolling motor. When we arrived at the lake, we began trolling casting big leech patterns behind the boat, jigging them up and down. No luck. About an hour after we arrived, the front blew in. The wind was howling. Joe said to us, "Folks, we could stay here and fish in the wind, but we won't catch anything because I can't control the speed of the boat." Fortunately, he had a back-up plan: We would head back to his ranch and fish the creek, which runs through it for rainbows.

Although Shaya and I were disappointed that we would not have a chance to catch a lunker, the rest of the day turned out to be fun. We drove back to his ranch where Joe picked up a rifle and we headed to the creek joined by his two Karelian Bear Dogs. Why the rifle and the Bear Dogs?

The answer, of course, is because of grizzlies. In pre-European times, grizzly bears roamed all over the West. As their numbers were reduced, the remaining populations were largely confined to the mountains. But in the last few decades, the grizzly bear population of northwestern Montana has expanded and so has their territory. They are once again out on the plains. Incidents between grizzlies and human beings are becoming more and more common. Just a few weeks before, a big grizzly had walked right behind Joe's wife as she was gardening.

Shaya with guide Jack Kip and his Karelian Bear Dogs. AUTHOR'S COLLECTION.

We caught a number of small rainbows on the creek and Joe showed me how to cast into a heavy wind—a technique I still use today. He also showed us a local buffalo jump where Indians had for centuries chased buffaloes over a cliff to their death before the Europeans introduced the horse to the Blackfeet, which made buffalo jumps obsolete. We also had a chance to talk. At one point, Joe asked me what I had done for a living. I said that I had taught American history at the college level. Joe asked me if I had paid attention to the Indians. I replied that I certainly had—which was the truth. In fact, while at Carroll College, as part of a cultural exchange program, a colleague and I had lived with five Carroll students on the Cheyenne River Indian Reservation in South Dakota. That clearly set Joe at ease. I have been surprised and appalled by the amount of prejudice against American Indians on the part of whites in northwestern Montana. Joe is not only a fishing guide but also a rancher. The day we fished with him he was busy selling his cattle, using his cell phone to close the deal as Shaya and I fished. The price he got for his cattle was good, so he was a happy camper. After we were finished fishing, we headed back to Joe's home where we met his wife and visited for a while. All in all a nice day, though I wish we had had a chance to fish for those monsters in Mission Lake which are reputed to be about the size of a submarine.

Fishing the reservation lakes on our own has been an adventure. When we first fished Duck Lake years ago, it was known for its big rainbows. It's a hard lake to fish from our kayak because it is big and windy. Most people who try their luck on Duck Luck usually are trolling from good-sized boats. We struggled, getting pushed this way and that by the wind and the waves. We did catch some nice sized rainbows, though, and I had a "close encounter" with one of the lake's behemoths. We were fishing in the fall when terrestrials are often the fly of choice. I had tied on an ant pattern. For a split second, I looked down at my reel for some reason. Big mistake. I heard a noise like someone jumping in the lake. But it wasn't a swimmer. It was a rainbow. It snapped my leader and was gone. I will never know if I would have hooked it had I kept my eye on my fly. I think there is a lesson to be learned here.

Hidden Lake is our favorite place to fish on the reservation. Though it's only about forty-five minutes outside of Browning down the Starr School Road, like Mitten, it's a sun-of-a-gun to find the first time you go looking for it. The nice thing about Hidden is that it is relatively small. Most of the reservation lakes are weedy, so there's lot of food in them, which is why the trout are big. Hidden is no exception. Because it is so close to Browning, the lake gets a good deal of pressure from the Blackfeet, as well as from serious fly fisherpersons who travel long distances to try their luck. I remember on one of our trips to Hidden Lake, we stopped to talk to one such fly fisher. In the back of his pickup truck, he had at least four fly rods ready to go with different rigs. So, if the fish were hitting dry flies, he could grab that rod; if they were hitting wet flies, he had a different rod and so on. Only problem was that he had not had much luck on the trip. Sigh.

On one of our excursions to Hidden, we were fishing leech patterns when we started to hear fish jumping around us. We could tell by the noise the splashes made that these were not ordinary size rainbows. Shaya decided to try a grasshopper pattern and made a cast. A giant rainbow leaped out of the water and grabbed it. The fight was on. I still remember the scene like it was yesterday. The trout dove deep down into the weeds only a few feet from the kayak. Shaya held on tight to it. I knew at the time this was a recipe for disaster—she had to set her drag and let the fish run. But I also knew from long experience to keep my mouth shut. On too many occasions, either a guide or I had shouted instructions to her when she had a good fish on the line. If the fish got away, there was hell to pay. Sure enough, the trout broke her line. It only took me a minute or two to tie on a grasshopper pattern. I began casting towards rising trout. Bang! A big one grabbed the fly. For once in my life, I played a fish well. I brought to net a beauty in the four-pound category. A nice trout but not a giant by Hidden Lake standards where rainbows in the eight-pound or more category are not uncommon.

Adventures Big and Small During Our "Golden Years"

Back into the "Bob" and Dave Brown's Stumptown Angler

Joe Kipp is not the only fly-fishing legend I have met in northwestern Montana. The other legend is Dave Brown ,who for years was the proprietor of the Stumptown Angler on Highway 93 just outside of Whitefish. It was a place where you could stop in to buy a few leaders or flies and spend an hour and a half talking fly fishing. People would wander in while I was talking to Dave (telling tall tales might be a more-accurate description) and soon they would be a part of the conversation. Or, I would wander in to join a conversation he was having with another fly fisher. After a few years, Shaya refused to go with me if I said I was driving over to the Stumptown Angler because she knew we could be in there a long time. There's something about most fly-fishing stores that bothers me: Most of them seem to have an officious atmosphere. Why this is, I don't know. Maybe it's because it's a sport that appeals largely to an elite clientele. In any case, I much preferred the ambience in the Stumptown Angler to any other fly shop that I have visited with the possible exception of the Austin Angler.

Dave liked to tell stories about how he had masterfully played big fish that he had brought to net. He also had a wealth of fishing knowledge that he was willing to share with his customers. One of the things he emphasized over and over is the importance of stealth when wade fishing. When

Dave enters a stream, he stands still for several minutes before beginning to cast. One of my favorite Dave Brown stories is about a wade-fishing trip he took with a friend on the Middle Fork of the Flathead River. There are several easy access spots on the Middle Fork along Highway 2 between West Glacier and East Glacier that Shaya and I have fished many times. But in many places the highway is several hundred feet above the river. You would have to be part mountain goat to access the river from such heights. But, somehow Dave managed to find a trail down the mountainside to a run that was loaded with big fish. So, one day, Dave and a friend made the arduous trek down the to the run. When the pair arrived, the put on their waders and got ready to fish. Apparently, Dave had neglected to tell his friend about the importance of stealth when wade fishing: The friend, who was ready to fish before Dave, stomped out into the middle of the run and began casting. After about ten minutes without a strike, he was mightily disappointed. Turning to Dave, he said, "There aren't any fish here." Disgusted, Dave replied: "Not anymore there aren't."

One of the proudest days of my life occurred in the Stumptown Angler. Shaya and I had just returned from our second trip into the Bob Marshall Wilderness Area. This was not primarily a fishing trip. Rather, it was a seven-day adventure on horseback to the "Chinese Wall," a limestone escarpment that runs along the Continental Divide unbroken for twelve miles and is about one thousand feet tall. We began the journey with our outfitter, Tom Parker, his trail hands, and four other guests from the Benchmark Trailhead about thirty miles west of the small town of Augusta. The total trip would be around seventy miles. To say that this was a challenge for me is an under-statement. The other guests were native Montanans. In fact, three of the four were from the same family: Grandmother, son, and granddaughter. All four guests had practically grown up on horses. The trip started out rather igno-miniously for me. Tom chose me to demonstrate how to properly mount a horse with his guidance. Unfortunately, the trail hand did not cinch the saddle correctly. When I attempted to mount the horse, the saddle slipped. I fell to the ground, banging my head. Fortunately, Shaya and I had decided to wear our bicycle helmets as protective gear. I was not injured. Tom looked at me lying on the ground and said, "Well, I never lost anybody in the corral before." Embarrassed, I dusted myself off and climbed aboard. The trail hand who had improperly cinched the saddle was sent packing by Tom the second day of the trip for refusing to follow Tom's orders. That left us short one trail hand.

I knew from past experience that there's nothing automatic about a trip into the "Bob." The third or fourth night out, after we had camped for the evening, the horses took off across one of the branches of the Sun River. Somebody had to go after them. Tom and a young trail hand, Cody, rode out to look for them as darkness approached. I was sitting in camp next to Cody's dad. I would have been a nervous wreck. He showed no emotion. Tom and Cody had walkie-talkies, but their communications kept breaking up because of the mountains. At one point, we heard one of them say that he had seen a grizzly bear. The two became separated. Tom finally found the horses, but by then it was dark. Would they make back to camp? Tom arrived first with the horses and the young trail hand a few minutes later: In the darkness he had followed the Sun River back to camp. Whew! The next day I talked to the dad, who admitted that he had been plenty nervous.

I did okay riding my horse. The only thing I did not like was when we had to stop. This happened frequently for one reason or another. For example, the mules that carried all the equipment and food could be stubborn. If a mule did not like the looks of a bridge that we had to cross, it would stop. The mule then had to be coaxed into moving again, which could take what seemed like an eternity. And I was not about to get off my horse unless I had to, so I would sit in the saddle and complain. The other guests confided in me that they felt the same way—only they were too proud to complain openly. Finally, we were within reach of the Chinese Wall. Tom told us in camp one night that in the morning, we would leave the horses behind and hike seven miles round-trip to the Wall. After complaining bitterly about all the horseback riding that I had had to do, I now took the opportunity to whine that I was going to have to hike. In the morning, the weather was glorious. We hiked to the Wall and were fortunate that ours was the only group there that day. It was a memorable experience. The next morning it was time to head back to the Benchmark Trailhead.

One major side trip remained, however: An arduous eleven-mile, round-trip horseback ride with a 3,380-foot elevation gain up a mountain to Prairie Reef summit which overlooks the entire Bob Marshall Wilderness complex. Spectacular views. But I had had quite enough of horseback riding by then. So, I decided to skip the trip and spend the day fly fishing. We had our fly-fishing gear with us and, in fact, early in the trip had caught some fish on the Sun River. Rebecca, one of the two naturalists on the trip and our camp chef, planned to stay in camp, so there would be someone around in case I got into trouble. Her boyfriend, Adam, the other naturalist (They are now married.), is also an expert fly fisherperson. I asked him what he would recommend using. He said, "Charles, try a Yellow Sally." Yellow Sallies are smaller stoneflies and are common in many streams across the county. How I happened to have some Yellow Sallies with me I do not remember. It's possible that Dave Brown told me have a few in my fly box for the trip. Or, perhaps, Adam gave me a few.

In any case, I donned my fly-fishing outfit and with fly rod in hand hiked the hundred yards or so from our camp down to one of the many branches of the Sun. It was one of those days where I did not expect to catch anything. It was just nice to be off my horse. The stretch of the Sun I was fishing was not big—perhaps fifty feet across. I tied on a Yellow Sally and tossed it out into the current. Bang! A rainbow grabbed the fly and took off. I was so thunderstruck that I did not react. The fish got away. I tossed out my fly again. Bang! Another rainbow attacked the Yellow Sally. This one did not get away. The run I was fishing was loaded with hungry rainbows eager to inhale my fly. I caught fifteen to twenty of them in the space of a few hours. They were all in the one- to two-pound category. Beautiful fish. For me, fishing days like this—when the unexpected happens—are always among the most memorable. Lord knows, they are rare enough.

That was not the end of the day's excitement, though. Just as I was about to head back to camp, Rebecca appeared on the bank of the river. She said, "Charles, don't hike through the woods on the way back to camp.

There's a bear in the area." She seemed unusually nervous. I said that I had not planned on going through the woods and that I would be back in camp shortly. She turned around and left. Later, I heard her story about the bear. The day was very warm—in the eighties. Rebecca was taking a nap in her tent, but it was too hot inside it. So, she decided to move her nap outside. She took a ground cloth from the tent and spread it on the ground in the shade and resumed her nap. The only problem—she forgot to take her bear spray with her. An hour or so later, she sensed something was amiss and awoke from her nap to see a young black bear no more than five feet from her. The bear seemed to be wondering whether or not Rebecca was a food item. She was terrified but made some noise and the bear ran off. Later I learned that young black bears who are not making it in the wilderness and are in danger of starving to death can be dangerous. The rest of the trip was uneventful and a few days later we were back in the Benchmark corral. After fond farewells, we headed back to Columbia Falls in the Highlander.

It did not take me long to head over to the Stumptown Angler after our return. I could not wait to tell Dave about my great day on the Sun River. A few weeks later, I was back at his shop again to buy some flies. When I walked in, Dave was conversing with three or four fly fishers. He introduced me by saying, "This is the guy who caught all those big rainbows on the Sun River." Naturally, I had to share with them all the details of my glorious day of fly fishing. They were duly impressed. I am surprised the buttons did not burst off of my shirt.

Unfortunately, the Stumptown Angler went out of business a few years ago. Originally, Dave's shop had been located on the main drag in Whitefish, but the town's growing popularity as a tourist destination meant that his rent kept increasing faster than his business could handle. So, he decided to move the shop to Highway 93 a few miles outside of town. It turned out to be a bad location. Dave lost almost all his walk-in business, which was considerable. Also, I had realized for some time that he was much better at talking about fly fishing with his customers than he was at operating his business. Nonetheless, I was shocked when I read in our local newspaper one day that the Stumptown Angler was having a going out of business sale. I rushed over to the store to say goodbye. A crowd was rummaging through the remaining merchandise. I was lucky to find an Orvis Stumptown Angler sweatshirt in my size. When some of the other longtime Dave fans who happened to be in the store saw what I had snatched up, they were jealous. I could have sold it on the spot for twice the reduced price. But, of course, I did not. It hangs in my closet in the Lodge. I am thinking about having it framed. Dave and I said our goodbyes. "I'll see you on the water" were our parting words to each other. There are plenty of other places to buy fly fishing supplies near our summer home, but it's just not the same.

Hiking Into Mountain Lakes

Driving to a mountain lake like Moose or Red Meadow is one thing; hiking to one is quite another. Indeed, one of my constant fishing frustrations over the years has been our limited hiking range. Northwestern Montana is home to many mountain lakes that have wonderful fishing, but most of them are a son-of-a-gun to get to. In many cases, they are only accessible to backpackers. So, I can only dream about what it would be like to fish for the large cutthroats or giant rainbows that inhabit their waters. Some lakes, though, are within our range. We have fished, for example, Stanton Lake, Avalanche Lake, Glacier Lake, and Dorris Lake.

Stanton is a pretty lake located off of Highway 2 in the Great Bear Wilderness. It's a four-mile, round-trip hike that begins with an ascent up a murderously steep hill but after that it's not bad. Shaya and I have wetted our fly lines in Stanton several times but have only caught small cutthroats. On one of our trips to Stanton we met the famous Over the Hill Gang hiking club in the parking lot. We had finished fishing and they had completed one of their legendary hikes. This group has breakfast together once every two weeks or so and decides on the spot where they are going to hike that day. Their hikes are always difficult, ranging from fifteen to twenty miles or more over mountainous terrain. One of them made the mistake of asking me how the fishing had been. Without missing a beat, I responded,

"We caught some six inchers and some little ones." He thought that my joke was hilarious. That made my day. My family has heard this corny joke so many times that they groan whenever I get a chance to tell it to some unwitting person.

The gorgeous Avalanche Lake hike is one of the most popular in all of Glacier National Park. It is about a five-mile, round-trip hike with only a modest elevation gain. Of course, if you wish to hike to the head of the lake where the fishing is reputedly the best, add another mile and a half. We met a young man who was an expert fly fisher at Swiftcurrent Lake years ago who told us that Avalanche had a healthy cutthroat population. He had caught a ton of them on a recent trip to the lake. "Fish the far side of the lake," he said, "where the creeks run into the water." So, off we went a few weeks later. The fishing was only mediocre, though. I caught a half-dozen or so small cuts. Shaya did not catch as many. This day stands out in my memory, however, because it is hard to imagine a more beautiful lake to fish in the Lower 48. Of course, on the way back to the trailhead, we saw a huge hatch taking place at the foot of the lake. Trout were jumping all over. Oh well, that's fishing.

Glacier Lake is another easy lake to access. The hike is only about three miles round-trip and is located in the Mission Mountains—another spectacularly beautiful area of northwestern Montana that receives much less traffic that Glacier National Park. To get there, we drive south from the tourist town of Bigfork down Highway 83 south to mile marker 38 where we turn west on to Kraft Creek Road. From there, it's eleven and a half miles to the trailhead. We each had a fly rod in hand on our last hike into Glacier Lake, which contains cutthroat trout. When we arrived at the lake, we started casting and began catching a few tiny trout—in the six-inch range. I was about to learn that even fishing mountain lakes that we can reach has its frustrations.

About an hour after we arrived, two young men showed up. They had hiked into the lake carrying float tubes. They quickly began assembling the float tubes and rigging up their hand-made fly rods. I quickly realized that these were hard-core trout fishermen. Naturally, I engaged them in conversation. They said they had fished Glacier Lake several times before and added that they were heading towards a sand bar that was a terrific spot for trout. "And how big are the trout out there," I asked. "About twelve inches or so?" Now, I don't know if you have ever seen one of my favorite movies, *Chinatown,* starring Jack Nicholson as "J. J. Gittes," a private detective who attempts to solve a mystery involving water rights and a murder in California. In one scene in the movie, Gittes drives out to an orchard to question a fabulously wealthy character named Noah Cross, played by the famous movie director, John Huston. Gittes asks Cross how much he is worth, guessing that he may be worth as much as one million dollars. When Cross hears Gittes' guess, he lets out a hearty guffaw and informs Gittes that he is worth many times that. The guffaw that the two fishermen uttered when I guessed how big the trout were could have been uttered by Huston. After they were finished laughing, they said, "On, no. They are much bigger than that. They're in the fifteen- to eighteen-inch range," adding that we would hear them whooping and hollering from the lake as they pulled in the fish. I had heard enough. They did give us one a tip, though, before they departed. "Try the creek on the way back out," they said. "It's got some big cuts in it." So, on their way out we tried the creek, which is no more than ten feet across. Shaya tossed her fly out into the current. A huge trout dashed out from under a log, grabbed the fly and broke her off within the space of a few seconds. We fished for a few more minutes but did not have any more strikes. So, we hiked back to the trailhead.

When we arrived back home, I was still green with envy. Determined to make it out to that sandbar, I ordered an ultra-lightweight float tube from an online company. It arrived about a week later. I strapped it on my back and began hiking around the yard. Alas, even though this was many years ago, I sadly realized that I was too old and infirm to carry the darned thing a mile and a half to Glacier Lake and back. So, I returned it. I still often think about how I might make it to the sandbar. My plan is to hire an outfitter who would carry our inflatable kayak by horseback to the lake. We would then inflate the kayak and take off. At an appointed time, the outfitter would meet us on shore where we would deflate the kayak, put it on the horse and hike back to the trailhead. However, my tendency to procrastinate has kept me from executing this plan.

Dorris Lake is off of the west side Hungry Horse Reservoir Road. It's a long ride of about eleven-mile ride up into the mountains before you reach the trailhead. In fact, the one time we fished this lake, we practically gave up trying to find it. Although the hiking book I was using mentioned that there was good trout fishing in Doris Lake, the directions to the lake that it gave were sketchy at best. Fortunately, we spotted a bow hunter walking along the road. Rolling down the window, we asked where the trailhead was. He informed us that the sign marking the Doris Lake hike was down but that the parking lot was just a mile or so up the road. A few minutes later, we were there. The hike to Doris Lake is about five miles round-trip. It starts out going down a big hill and then gradually climbs up to the lake. Actually, there are three Doris Lakes. We fished #1. When we arrived, fish were jumping—always a good sign. We each tied on a fly and began casting from shore. Shaya started catching a trout right away. They were nice sized fish for a small mountain lake, mostly in the ten to twelve inch category. I started catching some too, but she out fished me that day. Then about an hour after we arrived, the fish simply stopped going after our flies. The menu had changed. The water is so clear in Doris Lake # 1 that I could see the trout swimming by me in schools. If I had had a net with a long handle, I could have scooped them up from shore—they were that close to me. The trout were clearly eating something, but what it was I will never know. We tried all sorts of small flies to no avail. After about a half an hour, we called it quits and hiked back to the trailhead. Naturally, I asked the local fly fishing gurus what they though the trout were eating. The consensus was that it was something tiny just below the surface. I would like to make another trip into Doris Lake, but to date I have been unable to talk Shaya into going.

Golden Trout or Not Golden Trout? —That is the Question

I learned the hard way that if you are hiking to a lake that you think you might want to fish, take your fly rod with you. Several years ago, we were camped in the T@B at beautiful Holland Lake in the Swan Valley.

It was August and the fishing was awful: In fact, so awful that we had given up trying. "Let's do a hike tomorrow we have not done before," I said to Shaya. After consulting our hiking books, we decided to strike out for Crescent Lake in the Mission Mountains. The hike to Crescent Lake begins at the same trailhead as the hike into Glacier Lake, but after a mile and one half, you take the trail to the right. The total round-trip distance to Crescent is about seven miles. It's a hike we would not attempt to do today because it is moderately difficult and is in a remote area. At the time, though, it was within our range and I had my GPS with me so hopefully we would not get lost. I remember Shaya asking me if I thought we should take our fly rods with us. "Nah," I said, "it would be a waste of time. Let's just enjoy the hike."

In the morning, we made the long ride to the Glacier Lake trailhead, parked the Highlander and started hiking to Crescent Lake. After about a mile, we took Trail 690 and began traversing the eight switchbacks to the lake. I remember it being a little bit dicey in terms of exactly which way we were supposed to go, but the GPS helped because I could see Crescent Lake on the screen. After a few hours, we arrived at the shore of the lake. We both gazed off into the distance, admiring this absolutely gorgeous twenty-eight-acre lake. Then I looked down into the crystal-clear water. There were dozens of trout swimming around a few feet from shore! But they did not look like any trout that I had ever seen before. They looked, well, sort of golden. Now, of course, I wished that we had packed in our fly rods. But there was nothing we could do. We certainly could not hike back to the car to fetch them. So, we watched the fish swimming around for a few more minutes, had lunch, and started the hike back to the trailhead. All the way back down the trail, I kicked myself for being so stupid as to not bring at least one fly rod. In fact, all these years later, I am still kicking myself. Quite possibly the mystery trout would have turned up their noses at our offerings, but I will never know whether or not we could have caught some of them.

I had to investigate further whether these mystery fish, in fact, could have been golden trout. So, on the way home we stopped by the headquarters of Swan Valley Connections (though it had a different name back then), a wonderful local environmental organization located near the community of Condon. I asked the woman behind the counter if she knew if there were golden trout in Crescent Lake. She replied that she did not know but added that she knew someone who would. So, I gave her my email address and we departed. A few days later, the answer arrived in my inbox. The person who contacted me informed me that, yes, indeed, we could have been looking at golden trout. Years ago, he explained, the Montana Fish, Wildlife & Parks department stocked golden trout in some of the state's lakes. Although they had not been stocked directly in Crescent Lake, they had been stocked in the even more remote and seldom visited Heart Lake, located about a mile beyond Crescent. The two lakes are connected by Crescent Creek, so it's quite possible that during high water in the spring that some of the golden trout made their way down the creek from Heart to Crescent. Indeed, my forty-year-old guide to fishing northwest Montana states that fishing for golden trout in Heart was quite popular after the fish were first stocked in 1963. What really seals the deal, though, is the information provided by the Montana Fish, Wildlife & Parks website. Under "Fish Species" for Crescent Lake, it lists both "Golden Trout" and "Westslope Cutthroat Trout." In fact, the Montana government's "Field Guide" states that the golden trout is "a California species" that was first introduced in Montana in 1907. It adds

Golden trout. ILLUSTRATION BY B. W. EVERMANN, BULLETIN OF THE BUREAU OF FISHERS, CIRCA 1906, UNIVERSITY OF WASHINGTON.

that there are currently about twenty golden trout populations in the high mountain lakes of western and south-central Montana. Some weighing up to four pounds have been caught in Montana, but the typical size is six to twelve inches. The email I received from Swan Valley Connections ended with a cautionary note: Do not tell anyone that there's golden trout in these lakes because if you do there will be cars parked for miles up and down Highway 83 by trout fishermen eager to catch them. So, I must ask that you please keep this information under your hat (though anyone can find it who uses the Montana Fish department's excellent website).

Adventures at Clayton Lake:
We Meet Forest "Elves" and Narrowly Escape a Disaster

For several years, I had been hearing from several sources about the great cutthroat trout fishing in Clayton Lake. In 2009, the lake and creek were "treated" with rotenone (fish poison) to remove hybrid trout and were restocked with genetically purebred westslope cutthroat trout in 2010. Restocking worked as the newly planted westslope trout population began reproducing and growing to healthy sizes. Clayton is sixty-two acres in size and is over one hundred ninety feet deep. It is located in yet another spectacular area of northwest Montana—the Jewel Basin—which is located east of Kalispell and west of the Hungry Horse Reservoir. The Basin is over 15,000 acres and includes twenty-seven lakes and thirty-five miles of hiking trails. To get to most of the trailheads, you turn off of the Echo Lake Road and wind your way up the mountains for several miles to the parking lot at "Camp Misery." However, Clayton Lake is one Jewel Basin lake that is accessed from a different trailhead—you take the west side Hungry Horse Reservoir Road until you reach the Clayton Creek Road #1633. The six-mile, round-trip hike itself is rated as only moderately difficult. However, because the trail is lightly used, it is not as well maintained as the other trails in the Jewel Basin. This fact would come into play on our second hike to the lake.

Late in the summer many years ago, we decided to hike to the lake to try our luck. I remember the day well. It was sunny, very cool for the time of the year (even by Montana standards) and windy. Not a good fishing day—but we decided to go anyway. After a long ride up the west side reservoir road and a few more miles up the Clayton Creek Road, we arrived at the trailhead. Only a few cars were in the parking lot—probably backpackers heading into the Jewel Basin. That was a good sign. The hike proved somewhat more difficult than I thought it would be. For the first few miles, we were out in the open. I knew from previous hiking experience that this is not good because a hiker can quickly become dehydrated in the sun. But since the temperature was only in the fifties, it was not a big problem on this particular day. We had to watch our step even more than usual, however, because of the rough condition of the trail. After a while, we began the climb to the lake, plodding along a half dozen or so dreaded switchbacks. After a few hours, we arrived. Clayton Lake is not a particularly beautiful lake by Montana standards, but it is remote. So, I felt a sense of accomplishment at having reached it. I remember saying to Shaya, "Now this is wilderness!"

No sooner had I said this than I began to hear some noise. The more I listened the more it sounded like children singing. What the heck, I thought, who could be singing? The singing grew louder. I was dumbfounded. After several minutes, children began emerging from the forest on the trail just behind us. And they were singing. They must be forest elves, I thought. But, no, they looked like normal children ranging in age from maybe eight to twelve years old. Then a few adults emerged from the forest. Who could this group possibly be? When the children and adults reached us, I asked the adults who they were. "We're the home school organization from Columbia Falls," I was told. They explained that on every other Friday during the summer, they took the children on a hike into the wilderness. The kids seemed totally on unfazed by the hike that we had just struggled on. Now, Clayton Lake has an elevation of over 6,000 feet and it was cold up there that day. After we talked for a few more minutes, the group hiked to a point about a half mile down the lake. The boys and girls were wearing their swimming outfits under their clothing. So, after stripping down, they all proceeded to jump into the ice-cold lake while the parents built a bonfire on shore. Montana children: They are not mollycoddled like the children of "helicopter" parents in the cities.

But it was time to start fishing. In light of the conditions—cold and windy—we should not have caught any fish. But Clayton is so good that within a few minutes, we had each landed a few nice sized cutthroats, though none of the four pounders that allegedly inhabit the lake. We continued to catch more fish, but after about an hour and a half, we realized that it was time to head back to the trailhead. One of the problems with hiking into mountain lakes is that by the time you get there, you may have precious little time to fish. And, you may not be able to fish the best spots in the lake. I had been told, for example, that the fishing was really good behind a small island directly across from us. However, getting there might have taken us more than an hour. The other really good spot was at the head of the lake, but that meant hiking more than mile up the shoreline. Also not an option. So, we put away our fly rods and began the hike back to the trailhead. On the way, we met a woman on one of the switchbacks who was backpacking into the Jewel Basin. She was carrying one of the biggest backpack I had seen in a long while. On top of it was a checkered red and white tablecloth. She was sweating profusely, though the day was still chilly. "How far is it to Clayton Lake?" she asked, with a note of panic in her voice. I delivered the unhappy news to her that I thought she still had more than a mile to go. She thanked me and began plodding up the switchback. She looked so fatigued that Shaya and I wondered if she would make it to the lake.

Our initial foray to Clayton Lake left me feeling frustrated. It had been a terrible fishing day and yet we had caught fish. I wanted to return. At the time we did the hike, I figure was in my mid-to-late sixties. Shaya is two younger than me, so knock off a few years for her. We have never really been long-distance hikers, but since retirement we have managed to tackle some pretty demanding hikes. For example, we did the spectacular Iceberg Lake hike in the Many Glacier area of GNP. It's 9.3 miles round-trip with an elevation gain of 1,450 feet. Though it's shorter, we also did the even more challenging Scenic Point hike in the Two Medicine area of GNP.

It's 7.4 miles with an elevation gain of 2,352 feet. And, finally, there's the killer 6.2-mile Mount Aeneas Summit hike in the Jewel Basin with an elevation gain of 1,781 feet. So, we are fairly good senior-citizen hikers who try to stay in decent shape. But age invariably takes its toll, as we were about to find out.

During the summer of 2017, I began planning our return to Clayton Lake. If memory serves, Shaya was not so eager to go but I somehow managed to persuade her to give it a shot. Sometime in August, with the weather forecasters predicting that the next day would be sunny with a high in the seventies and relatively little wind, I decided now was the time. I packed the Highlander with our fishing gear the night before so we could leave relatively early (by our standards) in the morning. We made the repeat drive to the Clayton Lake trailhead, parked the SUV and began hiking. Bad news. The trail was in much worse shape than it had been before. It was overgrown and had numerous holes in the ground we could easily stumble on. We had to watch every step we took, which slowed us down. I remember tripping and hurting myself early on in the hike. We discussed turning around but decided to press on. The day was indeed sunny and much warmer than on our first hike. We had forgotten how exposed the early part of the hike was. It seemed like we would never make it to the shade of the mountain forest. Finally, we could see the lake. But then to complicate matters, I took a wrong turn on the trail and we had to retrace out steps to get to the shore.

We strung up our fly rods and began fishing in about the same place on our earlier trip. We started catching some cuts. After about a half an hour, we saw a young man emerging from the forest and walking towards us. This guy looked like the Hulk. He must have been about six foot four inches and two hundred and fifty pounds. He was carrying a fly rod in his hand and had a very large pistol strapped to his waist (a sure sign that he was a "local" rather than a tourist or transplant, both of whom carry bear spray). He walked up to us, said hello and then asked, "How did you folks make it up here?"

We replied, "What do you mean?"

"Well, he said, "it is as hot as hell in the sun on the first part of the hike," adding that a couple of hikers much younger than us had called it quits and turned around. We informed him proudly that we were both in our seventies and were in good shape. He said, "You two are an inspiration."

I swear that at the exact moment that he finished his sentence, Shaya fainted, falling onto the sharp rocks on the shore. Now, to this day, she claims that she did not pass out but simply became "disoriented" for a moment. However, the young fisherman and I both saw her eyes rolling around in her eye sockets. He picked her up where she lay and carried her to a grassy area. We saw that she had cut her arm badly and was bleeding profusely. She had also hit her head on the rocks (though we would not know that for certain until a few days later when a large black-and-blue bump appeared on her forehead).

We were in trouble. We had a demanding three-mile hike back to the trailhead in front of us and Shaya was in bad shape. I always carry a well-equipped first aid kit on our hikes. But before applying some disinfectant to her gashes and covering them with large Band-Aids, I decided to wash them off with some of our drinking water. In retrospect, this was probably a mistake since it would leave us desperately short of water on the way back down to the Highlander. The young man was very concerned about us. He said that he was going to hike up to the head of the lake where the big cuts were schooled up. After he was finished fishing in a few hours, he planned to return to the trailhead. He said, "If you can't make it, wait for me on the trail in the shade until I come along and I will make sure you get out of here." We thanked him profusely; assured him we would be okay and began walking. We were lying when we said that we would okay. The fact is that we were both badly shaken and were worried about our ability to get back to the trailhead. The hike back down the switchbacks was bad enough, but when we emerged into the sunlight it became pure hell. I had a brand-new GPS with me but was having trouble figuring out how to work the darned thing. So, I could not track how far we come and how far we still had to go. I knew we were going at a snail's pace. What is only a three-mile hike suddenly seemed to be a ten-mile hike. Somewhere along the way, Shaya twisted her knee, which slowed us down even more. And then my right leg began to give out. My muscles were failing—I was having trouble walking.

But Shaya and I both knew that we had an ace in the hole. It so happens that Flathead County has a wonderful rescue service. The Two Bear Air Rescue, based in Whitefish, provides world-class aviation support for search and rescue. It is provided free of charge to anyone by the Whitefish philanthropist Mike Goguen. Crazy though it may seem, we have discovered that we have cell phone service in some really remote areas of northwest Montana. And the Clayton Lake Trail is one of them. So, if we knew were deep trouble and did not want to wait for the young man to find us hunkered down the trail, we could call 911. Two Bear would come to the rescue. Here's the thing, though: We did not want to wind up as a story in our local newspaper, *The Daily Interlake.* I could imagine the headline: "Foolish Old Couple Attempts Demanding Clayton Lake Hike—Rescued by Two Bear" The embarrassment would be worse than any fate we might suffer on the hike back to the trailhead—well almost. After more than two hours, we were almost out of water and energy. With my right leg shot, I began whining, saying that I did not think I could go another fifty yards without collapsing; and Shaya was just about done in too. That's when we started to hear some noise in the woods behind us. "Great," we thought, "we are about to be finished off by a grizzly bear." Fortunately, at about the same time, I finally figured out how to work the GPS. Thank God! I could see the parking lot on the GPS's screen no more than a hundred yards away. We were saved! Within a few minutes, we were packing our fly fishing gear in the Highlander. Then the animal that had been making noise in the woods appeared: It was not a grizzly bear after all— just a large buck. We drove back to the main highway where I stopped in a convenience store to buy some Gatorade, which we both guzzled down.

That should be the end of the story but, alas, it is not. Shaya did not have any long-term damage from her fall, but I had seriously injured the adductor muscles in my right leg. It would take more than two years of on and off again physical therapy for me to strengthen the muscles to the point where they no longer bother me very much.

By now I am sure you are champing at the bit to hike into Clayton Lake where large cuts are just waiting to nail your fly. Well, good luck. Here's one review from the Internet dated July 2018:

> Awesome hike except that the trail was overgrown and some-one took a machete to it and left sharp blunt sticks into the trail which both my wife and I have huge scratches on our legs. I would recommend using soccer shin protectors. The fishing was great, 15-16 inch cuts that fight till the end. The hike was 1 h 45 m in and 1 h out from the hungry horse wear side res-ervoir road. Trail # 420 off Clayton Creek. Also recommend bear spray, we saw signs of Grizzly bears.

The problem with the Clayton Lake hike for us is that we had bitten off more than we could chew given our age and level of conditioning. As we grow older, the number off lakes and rivers in northwest Montana that we can still fish shrinks. Wade fishing in most places is now out of the question for Shaya with her arthritic knees. And I have serious reservations myself about continuing to wade fish. Is it worth risking breaking a hip, leg, or arm to catch some more trout? Last summer we did two wade fishing trips on the North Fork, but we only fished the first spot. We caught some nice cuts but nothing to write home about. The second spot, my favorite, we did not attempt to fish. As far as hiking to mountain lakes, at the present time we could still make it to Stanton, Avalanche, Glacier and a few others. But Clayton Lake, Dorris Lake, Crescent Lake and many others that I have dreamed about fishing are out of the question. And riding a horse again into the Bob Marshall Wilderness is beyond the pale. Of course, we are still able (knock on wood) to carry the inflatable kayak down the path to several lakes. So, we can continue to fish places like Red Meadow and Moose.

This diminution is inevitable. One of my favorite short stories is by the noted Texas author, John Graves, who is best known for his classic work, "Goodbye to a River." In this short story, the main character is fly fishing in a Texas Hill Country river. The current is stronger than he antic-ipated. He falls down, nearly drowning before struggling back to shore. The man realizes as a result of this experience that he has grown old. This story spoke to me when I read it several decades ago; it speaks to me even more now. The truth of the matter is that northwestern Montana is not an easy place to fish—especially for senior citizens. I have thought about selling our "lodge" outside of Columbia Falls and renting a cabin for the summer instead on one of the countless lakes in the Spooner area of north-west Wisconsin. The fishing would be more relaxed for us. We could have the fourteen-foot Lund equipped with a twenty-horsepower outboard and electric trolling motor tied up down at the dock ready go whenever we were. The fishing is good on these lakes for the warm water species that I pursued early in my life: perch, crappies, bass, walleyes and northern pike. And if Shaya and I were to have a desire to go trout fishing, there's plenty of that in the area too. But, of course, we will never do it. Northwest Montana is too breathtakingly beautiful to leave and after more than ten years in the area we feel at home there. Also, as we shall see later in this story, there's a wonderful place near the "lodge" where we will be able to fish for trout until late in our dotage.

The Smallmouth Bass Bruisers of Horseshoe Lake

Smallmouth bass are native to east-central North America but have been widely planted by hatcheries across the United States—including Montana. In fact, according to the Montana Field Guides, Horseshoe Lake was first water body in Montana to receive a stocking of smallmouth bass way back in 1914. Since then, it has been stocked repeatedly with smallies. Like so many lakes we have wound up fishing in northwest Montana over the years, I am not sure how I learned that Horseshoe was reputedly good lake to fish for the smallmouth. There's a good chance it was by listening to the weekly fishing report put out by the legendary Snappy Sports Center, founded in 1947, located in Kalispell. Snappy's is one of those "throw-back" places that have become all too uncommon these days. We love to stop by to purchase a few items and just look around.

Horseshoe Lake is located about eight miles south of Bigfork, which means it's about a forty-five minute drive from our "lodge." It is approximately forty acres in size with a maximum depth of thirty-one feet. The lake is mostly shallow and weedy and has only one deep hole located in a long, narrow bay. It is very much unlike the premier Minnesota smallmouth bass lakes I fished in my younger days, which tend to be deep and rocky. Why the smallmouth bass like Horseshoe Lake is something of a mystery to me. But there they are. Though we have never caught them in large numbers in this lake, the ones we catch tend to be big—a fact we discovered on our very first expedition. We had been on the lake for perhaps a half an hour, working our way down the weedy right shoreline. I don't remember what I was fishing but Shaya had a flashy minnow imitation attached to the end of her fly line. She was stripping in her line when she said to me, "I'm stuck on the bottom." At first, I thought she was right. Then I took a closer look at her fly line. It was definitely moving through the water. I said to her, "You aren't stuck. You have a fish on the line." I had no sooner finished my sentence when a gigantic smallmouth came leaping out of the water. We could not believe our eyes at what we had just witnessed. We both let out a let out a collective gasp. The battle was on. After a several minutes, I managed to net Shaya's fish. It easily weighed four pounds. That was the first of many huge smallmouth bass we have landed in Horseshoe Lake. Mostly, they have fallen prey to leech patterns bounced along the bottom of the lake. I would be less than honest, though, if I were not to admit that on many trips to Horseshoe Lake, we fail to get a strike. This is especially frustrating because we almost always see several bruisers swimming along below the surface.

And even when we are lucky enough to hook a big smallmouth bass on our fly rods, they are not so easy to catch. In the summer of 2020, we arrived in Montana in mid-July—about six weeks later than usual due to the pandemic. It was already past prime time for fishing Horseshoe, but Shaya wanted to make at least one trip to the lake. So, we packed up the Highlander and departed for Horseshoe later in the morning than we normally would. My heart was not really in to the expedition. I was convinced we would get skunked. When we put the kayak in the water, we paddled down to the narrow bay with the deep hole and began tossing our leeches into the water. Now, I believe that I am a much better fisherman when I am expecting to catch fish than when I am not. This is all in the way of making an excuse for what happened next. On about my thirtieth cast, my line stopped in the water. A smallmouth had grabbed it. I have sparred you the stories of my fly-fishing expeditions for bonefish in Belize. I remember well the first time I tied into one. My mouth fell open as the fish stripped about one hundred feet of line off my reel in a matter of a few seconds.

I will not pretend that this smallmouth bass matched that bonefish, but it was very reminiscent of the experience. We were in open water in the narrow bay and the line went whizzing off my fly reel at an incredible pace. I was surprised and caught totally off guard. This was one time that I wished I had had an experienced guide with me in the kayak because the guide would have said to me, "Charles, set your drag and let the fish run." But since there was no guide, I did an utterly foolish thing. I attempted to stop the bass. The leader snapped and the fish was gone. When I check out what had happened, I discovered the leader had broken where I had tied on some tippet material. And, of course, the tippet material was way too light for a fish that strong. I could have cried. God knows how big that smallmouth bass was. What really troubles me is that I will never know. If I am going to lose a big fish, I at least like to get a look at it. Maybe next summer we will have a rematch. If so, I will be prepared.

Me with a big smallmouth bass, Horseshoe Lake.
AUTHOR'S COLLECTION.

Pine Grove Pond: The Last Place We May Ever Fish for Trout

Several years ago, Cam and I were talking about places to go fishing. I was complaining to him about how it was becoming increasingly difficult for Shaya and me to access some of our favorite spots due to our increasing age. After listening to me kvetch for a while, Cam said, "When don't you try the kids' pond?" Now, the "kids' pond" is actually the Pine Grove Pond—a five-acre body of water located three miles north of Kalispell just off of Highway 2. This means it is about a twenty-minute drive from our lodge. Anyone can fish Pine Grove but only kids under age fifteen are allowed to keep one fish. Montana Fish, Wildlife & Parks routinely stocks the Pond. To be honest, as an accomplished fly fisher (hah, hah), I was a little bit taken back that Cam had suggested that I should try my luck at a children's fishing pond. But I knew that he and his daughter, Hana, who at the age of five was already fly fishing, often went there. So, after the third or fourth time, he suggested it to me, I thought, "Why not give it a try?" One morning, Shaya and I packed the fly fishing gear in the Highlander and drove off to the pond.

Pine Grove Pond was originally a quarry owned by the Street family, who homesteaded in the Flathead Valley in 1883. The name "Pine Grove" comes from the school that the family founded on their 160-acre property. It was Robin Street, the current owner of the property, who had idea to build a family fishing pond at the quarry. The pond was four years in the making and would not have been possible without his donation of thirteen acres of land. We often met Robin when fishing at Pine Grove. He would drive down to the pond in his pickup truck, coffee cup and donut in hand. Rolling down the window, he would ask us how we were doing. And we would always give him a brief fishing report. It was obvious that seeing people fishing at the pond gave him great pleasure. Alas, Robin died at the age of eighty-five. Shaya and I attended a memorial service for him at the pond in March 2019.

I could not have been more flabbergasted by what we were about to experience. You know the drill with kids' fishing ponds: The fish stocking people throw a bunch of eight-inch put-and-take trout into the water.

Shaya fishing Pine Grove Pond. AUTHOR'S COLLECTION.

They usually do not put up much of a fight when hooked and generally look anemic when landed. Although to be sure there are plenty of small trout in Pine Grove, we were about to find out that the pond contains some impressive bruisers. I can think of two reasons for this. First, Montana Fish, Wildlife & Parks dumps lots of rainbows in Pine Grove that already weigh between one and two pounds. And they also stock some enormous "brood" fish that that range between eight and eighteen pounds. The "FishMT" stocking reports for Pine Grove tell the story. For example, in the year 2014 (which is about when I believe we first started fishing at Pine Grove) they released ninety-five rainbows that were at least twenty-seven inches, seventy-five that were twenty-one inches and more than five hundred fifty that were fifteen inches or bigger. In addition, they stocked several thousand smaller trout. The second reason is that the trout actually grow in Pine Grove due to favorable conditions. An underground river flows beneath the pond keeping it rich in nutrients and fresh water. And its maximum depth is seventeen feet, providing enough oxygen for fish to survive through the winter months.

We noticed some trout jumping as we pulled up at the pond. And they did not appear to be the put-and-take trout of the eight-inch variety that we had expected. Some of them appeared to be quite large. So, we tied on some dry flies and began making casts. If memory serves, I had a large stimulator on my line and made some casts towards a rising fish.

A big rainbow jumped out of the water and grabbed the fly. After a furious brief fight, I landed the fish. It easily weighed two pounds. That was the first of dozens of big rainbows that Shaya and I caught that first year at Pond Grove on dry flies. And it wasn't just rainbows that we caught. The FishMT people had also stocked some nice sized cutthroats. I remember standing on the shore at the south end of the pond catching one twelve-inch cutthroat after another on elk hair caddises.

The Day of the Monster Trout

To be honest, I do not remember whether it was the first year or the second year that we were fishing Pine Grove that I hooked a monster trout. I do remember that I was fishing the east shore of the pond when something big grabbed my fly. It took off across the pond like the proverbial submarine. I set the drag on my reel and let it run. After what seemed like an eternity, the fish started to tire, and I began slowly reeling it in. It made several more runs before I finally had it close to the shore. When the trout finally surfaced about three feet from shore, I almost fainted. It was enormous— by far the biggest rainbow I had ever had on my line. By this time, I had attracted a small crowd of children who were watching me fight the fish. I did have a net on the back of my fishing vest, but it was useless since I needed one suitable for landing a redfish or muskie. Shaya was fishing off a pier on the other side of the pond and I remember yelling at her that I had a big fish on the line. There wasn't anything she could do to help me land the fish, but she did have a camera, which, as it turned out, would have come in handy had she trotted over to my side of the pond. The kids and I were all trying to figure out to do when the fish made one last dash, broke the line, and was gone. So, I did not land the fish and I do not

have a photo of it. What I do have is the memory of the giant rainbow in the water only a few feet away from me. In retrospect, I can't think of anything that might have worked. Maybe I could have jumped in the pond and tried to grab it, but I think that would have ended in disaster. Dare I count this rainbow, which probably weighed somewhere around twelve pounds, as one I caught or as one that got away at the shore? I think I know the answer to that, so please don't tell me. I do have a photo of one that Hana hooked at landed at the pond with the help of her dad. I believe the one I failed to land was much bigger.

Hana and her monster trout.
AUTHOR'S COLLECTION.

Shaya and I began making regular trips to the Pine Grove Pond—sometimes on the order of twice a week. By this time, we were regularly using leech patterns to catch trout when the fish were not feeding on the surface. We also began noticing "regulars" who fished the pond as much as we did. One gentleman, in particular, caught our attention because he often pulled in two or three trout for every one that Shaya or I caught. He liked to fish from a rock on the east side of the pond. We often waved to each other. Finally, one day, I screwed up courage and walked over to him to introduce myself. It turned out his name was John and that he hailed from Augusta, Georgia. John had been fly fishing since childhood and he is an expert who ties his own flies. He gave Shaya and me a couple to try. We began talking about fishing the pond and swapping stories about our past fishing experiences. John and his wife, Peggy, soon became good friends with whom Shaya and I enjoy socializing. Shaya and I have named the rock from which he likes to fish "John's rock" in his honor.

The Old Gentleman in the Overalls

Although John is easily a few levels above Shaya and me in terms of his fly-fishing expertise, the three of us encountered an elderly fly fisher at Pine Grove the likes of whom none of us had ever experienced. When we first spied the old gentleman, he was dressed in overalls and was fishing from the pier on the west side of the pond. We noticed that he was catching trout one after another. Okay, John, Shaya, and I have all had some pretty good days at the pond, but nothing like this in terms of the number of trout the old gentleman was landing. It was nothing short of astonishing. John was the first among us to talk to talk to him. When we saw John again, we asked him what fly the old man was using. John replied, "It's a double renegade." We were puzzled. A renegade is one of our "go to" flies but it is a surface fly that may be fished subsurface. It is definitely not a fly that you bounce along the bottom. If memory serves, the old gentleman gave John one.

The next time Shaya and I saw the old gentleman fishing from the pier, he was still pulling in trout like nobody's business. I walked over to parlay with him. I asked him what he was doing to catch so many trout. In fact, while I was talking to him, he caught several and demonstrated for me his technique to entice them to strike. He also showed me the fly he was using and said it was a "double renegade." But it was nothing like the renegade that we were accustomed to using. In fact, it was a double beaded wet fly. He did not offer to give me one, so I asked him if it would be okay if I snapped a few shots of the fly. He said, "Sure." So, I took out my iPhone and took some pictures. On my way home, I stopped by Bob Arens' fly shop to show Bob the photo of the "renegade" and ask to Bob if he tie one for me. Bob said he would give it a try and that I should stop back in a few days and he would show me a few samples. A few days later, I was back in his fly shop. The flies were pretty darned close to the ones the old gentleman was using. After I paid Bob, Shaya and I rushed off to the kids' pond to try them out.

Now one of my favorite folk songs is about an old violin that comes up for auction. The auctioneer plays a few notes on the violin and asks who will pay a dollar for it. There's not much interest until a man in the back of the room walks up to the front and begins playing the violin masterfully. In fact, he plays it so well that people start crying. The violin that could not originally fetch one dollar sells for over a thousand dollars. People are astounded and can't understand what has just happened. The song explains that it was the "touch" of the "masters hand" playing the old violin that made the difference. I am afraid that the same was true for fishing the double renegade. To be sure, it turned out to be a good fly for us and one that I still have in my fly box. But the double "renegade" needs the touch of the "master's hand" to be truly a killer fly. Moral of the story: It's not just the fly—it's the fly fisher too.

Unfortunately, the first few years at Pine Grove were the best. After that, the fishing was still good but much tougher. There were increasingly more days where Shaya and I would only catch one or two rainbows or get skunked altogether. John even reported to us that he had seen the old gentleman in the overalls having a tough go of it. So, it falls into the same category as Barton Creek and Swiftcurrent Lake—bodies of water that were wonderful the first few years I fished them and then went into something of a decline. Perhaps with Pine Grove, it is because the fishing pressure grew considerably as more and more people became aware of what a special place it is. In the first few years, Shaya and I often fished the pond on weekdays when only a few other fisherpersons were present. That's not true anymore. Still, it is a terrific place for kids and seniors alike to fish. It may be the last place that we will ever fish for trout. Not a bad way to end one's fly-fishing career.

The Decline of the West

I previously mentioned that during the first year we were married, 1970, Shaya and I made a month-long journey from Chicago up to Minnesota and then across Canada Highway 1 all the way from Ontario to British

Columbia. Along the way we picked up a couple of hitchhikers, a young man and woman who were on their way to meet friends on an island in British Columbia, a mile or two off the mainland. In that time period, it was common for young Canadians to hitchhike back and forth across their beautiful country. They helped us with the long drive through the Canadian Provinces. When we got to the coast, we threw the Montgomery Ward SeaKing into the ocean, stuffed Budger the cat into a large bag ,and navigated our way out to the island where we stayed for several days. I remember catching rockfish of the shore that we had for dinner. When it was time to head back to Chicago, we drove through Washington, Idaho, and Montana.

In 1970 the Western Provinces of Canada and the American West were wild compared to today. In fact, today when we return to places we visited then, we are often in shock. Fifty years of development has made a huge difference—one that makes us sad. I remember on our way home driving through a remote area of Montana, surrounded by mountains as the sun was beginning to set, wondering if we would ever come to any sign of civilization. Finally, we came to a crossroads. In front of us appeared a saloon. But this was not just any saloon. It was the famous Silver Dollar Bar. In those days, the walls of the bar were lined with10,000 donated silver dollars with the names of the donors written under each coin. Today, it has more than 50,000. The bar is located in Haugan, an unincorporated community located sixteen miles east of the Idaho border and about ninety miles west of Missoula. It was a surprise to find this place in the middle of nowhere! We were tired, and the bar had camping out back, so we pitched our tent for the night. Today, the bar is still there, except now it is located on Interstate 90 at Exit # 16. It is still by all accounts a fun place to visit, but every time we are traveling on Interstate 90 and pass the bar, we feel a sense of loss. It now comes across as just another tourist attraction.

And Bozeman, Montana, located close to Yellowstone National Park, was the proverbial sleepy college town when we passed through it on our way home. It had a few motels, some restaurants, a bunch of bars and several fly-fishing shops. The city had a population in 1970 of maybe 15,000 people. When we visited it again in the early 1980s on our way to

Glacier National Park, it still was much the same. But by 2020, it had been transformed. According to census statistics, the metropolitan population of Bozeman in 2020 was pushing 120,000. It has become major tourist mecca for vacationers from the East Coast and the West Coast. You have to call a day ahead to make a reservation to dine at one of the town's many fine gourmet restaurants. Urban sprawl is encroaching on the surrounding mountains and rush hour traffic is bad. As the rent has gone up in downtown Bozeman, the fly-fishing shops have had to move off the main drag. If I were to write a review of modern day Bozeman, it would be entitled "There's no Montana left in Bozeman."

The same is true for Coeur d'Alene in Idaho. When I was a child growing up in Chicago, I dreamed of journeying to remote places like lakes Coeur d'Alene and Pend Oreille. I imagined men and women clad in heavy flannel shirts arising early in the morning to toss big plugs with their South Bend bait casting rods and reels in hopes of catching a monster northern pike. I imagined them returning to their pine log cabins before heading out to have dinner at the lodge. And when we visited the town of Coeur d'Alene in 1970, that's pretty much the way it was. Several years ago, Shaya and I rendezvoused in Coeur d'Alene with our good friends, Megan and Sam, who reside in Seattle. It had been a long, long time since I had visited Coeur d'Alene. There wasn't anything left in the town that one could describe as "rustic." Instead, chain stores that cater to tourists line the streets. The fancy Coeur d'Alene resort rises high over the lake. Unless I knew that I was in Coeur d'Alene, I might think I was in Miami. Coeur d'Alene is now a suburb of Spokane connected by an Interstate. Of course, what has happened in the West is not limited to the West. One of the memorable Zucker family vacations in the 1950s was to Gatlinburg, Tennessee, known as the gateway to Great Smoky Mountains National Park. We stayed in a delightful cabin with a burbling stream behind it. Gatlinburg back in the 1950s was a charming little town. Shaya and I drove through Gatlinburg about ten years ago on our way to visit her relatives in North Carolina. I couldn't believe it. Hideous tourist attractions line both sides of the main boulevard for miles. The place has become an abomination. I could not get out of there fast enough.

Of course, it is not just the towns that have changed in the West. It is the rivers too that have changed—and not for the good. The Madison River is a prime example of this. Of course, people fished on the Madison in 1970, but there was relatively little traffic on the river. I remember camping near the Madison on our way home. One evening Shaya and I took a hike after dinner with our cat (he liked to go on hikes with us, though he complained all the way) along the shore of the Madison. I recall thinking that I should try fishing it but did not have a clue as to what to do. I don't think we saw another person on that hike. How things have changed. On one of our excursions out west (circa 2010) after I retired, we decided to fish the Madison. We were staying in an RV campground about an hour from the river. So, we got up early in the morning and drove out to Ennis where we stopped in one of the town's many fly shops to inquire about the fishing. "Our fly-fishing school did pretty well at the Three Dollar Bridge yesterday," the shop proprietor informed us. So, after making the obligatory purchase of recommended flies, we headed out.

About forty-five minutes later, we arrived at the bridge. Now, I did not expect this to be a wilderness fishing adventure. I thought that perhaps since it was a weekday, there might be only five or ten vehicles in the parking lot. Wrong. It was more like thirty or forty. My mouth fell open. We discussed whether we wanted to stay or not. "What the hell, we're already here. Might as well give it go," we decided.

So, we got out of our car and began to don our gear. I looked around me. Perhaps a dozen or more other fly fishermen were getting ready to fish as well. They did not look happy and excited like most people do when they are about to begin fishing. In fact, they looked positively grim. Like they were getting ready to go into battle. Maybe because of the crowd they were in a hurry to get down to the river. Or maybe because they take fly fishing too seriously. In any case, we trekked down to the river where combat fishing was the order of the day. Fly fishers were spaced out about every fifty yards. Nobody was catching much of anything. Shaya tied on a gaudy wet fly, tossed it out into the water behind a rock and, of course, immediately hooked a three-pound rainbow. She landed that one. And then lost another big one a few minutes later. I got skunked. We stayed about an hour and then left.

Things on the Madison have only gone from bad to worse. In the summer of 2019, we did an auto tour from Columbia Falls where our summer home is located. We drove over the incredibly beautiful Beartooth Mountains to Cody, Wyoming. From Cody, we traveled west along the Shoshone River to the eastern entrance to Yellowstone National Park. (By the way, in my opinion, this is one of the most beautiful rides you can take in the United States.) We drove through the park and spent the night in West Yellowstone. The next day we found ourselves driving north along the Madison. "Let's just take a look at one of the put ins" I said to Shaya. "I am curious to see how crowded it is." Nothing could have prepared me for what I saw. Drift boats were lined up for blocks waiting to depart. On the river itself, the boats were practically playing bumper tag. It was astonishing. No thanks. How bad has it become? Outdoor writer Jim Robbins published a long piece in the November 23, 2020, edition of the New York Times detailing the mayhem on the Madison. Robbins notes that one writer in an outdoor wilderness journal coined the term "Rivergeddon" to refer to the situation. And it's not just fishing. Hiking trailheads and campgrounds in the Bozeman area have been overwhelmed too.

One of the reasons that Shaya and I chose northwest Montana for a summer home is because we figured we would be away from the crowds that were already plaguing less remote areas. And to a considerable degree that has been true, but things are beginning to change rapidly in our neck of the woods. Glacier National Park, located fifteen miles from our "lodge," is a prime example. Shaya and I still enjoy visiting Glacier to hike, bike, kayak and fish. But recent years the crowds in the park have become staggering, making it difficult to go. According to statistics compiled by the National Park Service, in 1982 when we visited Glacier with our friends, the Rosenthals, the Park had about 1.66 million visitors. By 2017, the highpoint so far for visitations, Glacier saw about 3.30 million people pass through its gates. So, over a period of thirty-five years, the number of visitors basically doubled. Interestingly, Glacier struck me as crowded in

1982; but, of course, the crowds back then are nothing compared to what they are today.

Let me give a few examples. Three or four years ago, Shaya and I made one of our pilgrimages to Swiftcurrent Lake to fish for brookies. The lake is located in the Many Glacier area of the park—the jumping off point for the hike to Grinnell Glacier. Hikers want to do this spectacular twelve-mile hike (we did it back in 1982) now more than ever because the glacier will be gone in another decade due to global warming. We drove by the area where hikers had parked their vehicles before striking out for the trailhead. We counted over a hundred. The Going-to-the-Sun Road is another example. This is arguably the most scenic drive in the United States. It takes about an hour and one half to wind your way up the road from the entrance to the park at West Glacier to the parking lot at Logan Pass. In recent years, the parking lot has become a madhouse with vehicles racing around desperately trying to find a spot. A few years ago, I asked a Park Ranger if it was legal to sell my parking spot to the highest bidder when we were ready to leave. I was kidding, of course, but she took me seriously and said, "The parking lot belongs to the government." (I know I could have made twenty bucks.) These days you had better be at the West Glacier entrance to the park by 5 am if you hope to find a parking spot at Logan Pass. And finally, there's the hamlet of Polebridge and its Bakery & Mercantile located up the North Fork Road. The first time I visited Polebridge, it was a remote place. But it is not any more. Now it has become a "must do destination" for visitors to the park. For years when Shaya and I would drive through the park on our way to fish the North Fork, we would see maybe three or four vehicles parked in front of the Mercantile. Today, the average is around twenty. I am happy for the new owner of the business who is making some money, but something has been lost. Eventually, I fear that developers will buy the Mercantile, rip it down and build a condo resort named "The Retreat at the Old Mercantile." I hope that I am not around to see it happen.

The problem is that you can't create more wilderness. When there's demand for a new Disney World, it's just a matter of coming up with the money to construct the place and then to build it. Glacier National Park is not any larger than when it was created back in the early twentieth century. And the Park Service is not about to build new campsites in it or roads through it. The same is true for blue-ribbon trout streams. The traffic on the main stem of the Flathead River has increased considerably in recent years. Though the far reaches of the North Fork remain lightly fished by today's standards, I fear that the "overflow" from rivers like the Madison and other rivers will soon change that. I know what you are thinking. "Aren't you and Shaya part of the problem. The answer to that question is indisputably, "Yes, we are." But that admission does not stop me from longing for a bygone era

Reeling in My Line One Last Time

When I started this project, I knew that I wanted to write about my fishing experiences over the last seventy years. I did not have any preconceived notions, really, of what I would discover about the role that fishing has played in my life. I was surprised by what I learned: Namely, that fishing has played a much bigger role in my life than I had ever imagined. Many of my most cherished memories, it turns out, revolve around fishing from my early childhood years in northern Wisconsin to my advanced senior citizen years in northwestern Montana.

What also became obvious to me is that most of these fishing experiences have been shared with family members and friends. First, there is my brother, Joe, with whom I shared a passion for fishing. Why my brother and I love fishing so much remains something of a mystery. My dad's big passions were the Chicago Cubs and betting on the ponies at Arlington Park. He probably never thought that when he met my mother that he would find himself rowing his boys around Summit Lake. My theory is that there's a fishing "gene" that has not yet been discovered. As I mentioned, my grandfather, Noye Pride, loved to fish (and hunt). Neither of my boys, Noah and Sasha, has shown much interest in fishing. I attribute this to the fact that Shaya and I made them sit in a canoe as children in a driving rainstorm on East Bearskin Lake because the smallies were biting like crazy. I can still remember them pleading for us to stop fishing and paddle to shore, Two of my five grandchildren love to fish, though; so, maybe the "gene" skips a generation now and then. Joe would eventually become known as the "Walleye King" on the North Shore of Minnesota. And after he moved out to East Hampton on Long Island, he became an expert salt-water fisherperson pursuing striped bass, sea bass and other game fish in his off shore boat.

My other major fishing partner, of course, is my wife, Shaya, whom I have known for over fifty-five years. I tried to remember when was the first time we picked up rods and reels to go fishing together but I do not recall it. My first strong recollection of fishing with her was casting for Coho salmon off the shore of Lake Michigan. I am guessing that fishing expedition took place around 1970—more than a half century ago. Although I was the one who initially took up fly fishing, she quickly followed suit. In fact, many years ago, I presented her with a four-weight Temple Fork fly rod for our wedding anniversary. She was very exciting about the gift and told several of her female friends about it. At first, they assumed that the "four weight." must refer to some kind of jewel and were puzzled to learn that it was a fishing rod. It's no surprise that Shaya loves to fish because both of her parents—as well as the extended family in North Carolina—loved to fish. Who's the better fisherperson between the two of us? You might get a different answer from her than me, but I think it's pretty much a toss-up. She has her own unique style of fly fishing, but it works. She consistently out fishes me when we are in the inflatable kayak. (I would like to think that this is because I am "guiding" from the back of the kayak). However, I think I hold the edge when it comes to wade fishing, perhaps because I am taller and somewhat stronger, so I can get farther out in the current. Do we always get along when we are fishing? Of course, not. When we are out on a lake, we often vociferously disagree about what spot to try next. And if Shaya loses a big one, look out—especially if I forgot to bring the net. But we have also learned to cooperate—sharing flies, etc. We have even developed our own sign language when we are wade fishing to let each other know what fly we are using. For example, holding my hands over my head and moving them up and down (like putting on a crown) is a sign that they are hitting a royal coachman. I am afraid I can't share with you the sign for using a stimulator.

The excitement of catching fish, of course, is the primary reason that fisherpersons go fishing—and that is certainly true for me. I have wonderful memories of the days out on a lake or stream when I brought to net a big fish or caught a whole bunch of beauties. But, as said earlier in this journal, it is the adventures that I had and the people that I met along the way that make my seventy years of fishing truly memorable. I am hoping that I still have time to make more memories, but I also know that not too far down the road is the last time that I will reel in my line.

Tight Lines!

Acknowledgments

One of the great joys of writing this book was communicating with friends and family about my fishing experiences over the last seventy years. My brother, Joe, with whom I spent much of the first forty years of my angling experiences, was a source of invaluable information. In many enjoyable phone conversations, we reminisced about our angling expeditions back in the good old days. I was lucky to marry a woman, Shaya, whose passion for fishing perhaps exceeds my own. Writing this book meant that she had to hear me tell again many of the angling stories that she had heard countless times before ("Remember the time, we were paddling across Duncan Lake when those smallies the size of footballs were biting in the rain?") Getting in touch with John Reiger, a buddy from graduate school days, was an unexpected bonus. We had not communicated with each other for over fifty years until we reconnected via the Northwestern University History Department newsletter. After that, we started swapping fishing stories via the Internet. Amazingly, he had photographs of our fishing outings together dating back to the 1970s. Proofreading is not one of my strengths. I was lucky to have two excellent volunteer proofreaders scrutinize this manuscript: My neighbor in Columbia Falls, Arlis Dailey, and my son, Sasha Zucker. Finally, the people at Sweetgrass Books did an incredible job polishing up the manuscript. Any mistakes, of course, that may remain are the responsibility of the author.

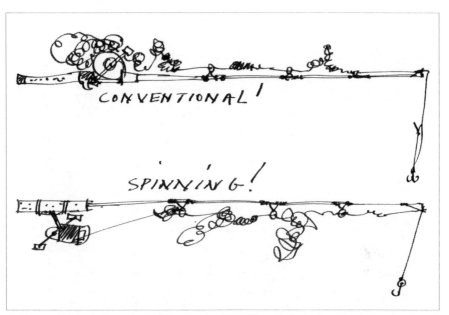

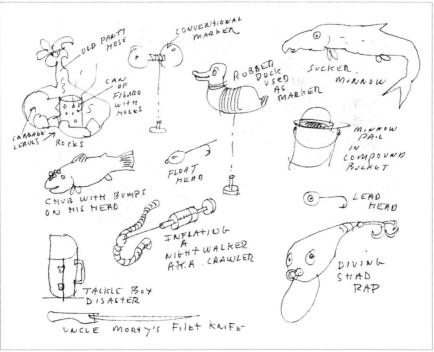

DRAWINGS BY "WALLEYE JOE" ZUCKER, TOFTE JOURNAL, NOLAN/ECKMAN GALLERY (1994).

Postcript, June 2022.
I landed this big cutthroat on Lake Rogers on a size 16 black zebra midge.
PHOTO BY CAM HOUSTON.

About the Author

Charles Zucker was born and raised on the south side of Chicago. His family annually spent its summer vacations in northern Wisconsin where his mother was reared. It was on one of these vacations more than seventy years ago that with his father and his brother, Joe, he first wet a line in beautiful Summit Lake. That began a life-long love of fishing that continues to this day. Zucker received his bachelor's degree from the University of Wisconsin and a Ph.D. in history from Northwestern University. After teaching at Fayetteville State University (North Carolina) and Carroll College (Waukesha, Wisconsin), he segued into professional association work representing college professors. He retired as the director of the Texas Faculty Association in 2007. After living in Austin for more than thirty years, he and his wife, Shaya, moved to San Antonio in 2019 where they currently reside.

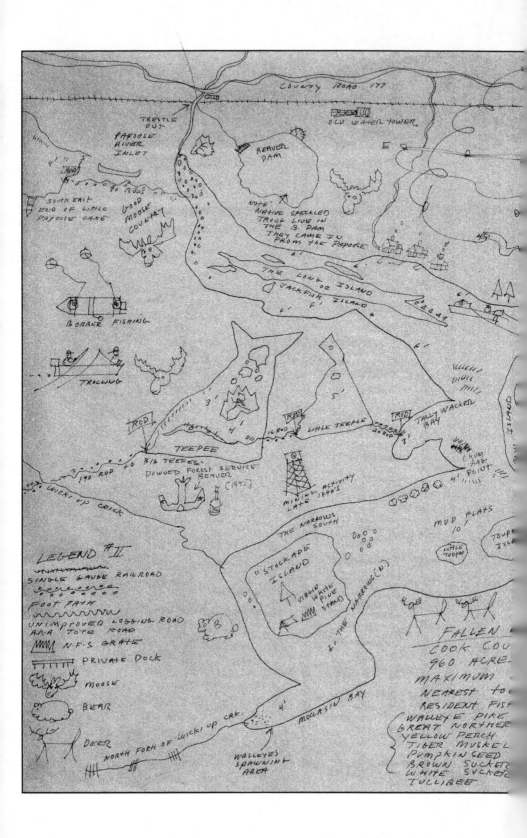

COUNTY ROAD 177

TRESTLE OUT
PAPOOSE RIVER INLET

OLD WATER TOWER

BEAVER DAM

E

SOUTH EAST END OF LITTLE PAPOOSE LAKE

GOOD MOOSE COUNTRY

NOTE:
NATIVE SPECKLED TROUT LIVE IN THE B. DAM
THEY CAME IN FROM THE PAPOOSE

THE LONG OR ISLAND

JACKFISH ISLAND

BORDER FISHING

TROLLING

ROD

ROD

LITTLE TEEPEE

ROD

TALLY WACKER BAY

CHUM BAY POINT

TEEPEE

B/G TEEPEE

DOWNED FOREST SERVICE BEAVER (1957)

190 ROD

WICKI UP CRICK

MINING ACTIVITY LATE 1890'S

THE NARROWS SOUTH

MUD FLATS 10'

LITTLE TOUPAD

TOUPA ISLAND

LEGEND #II

SINGLE GAUGE RAILROAD

FOOT PATH

UNIMPROVED LOGGING ROAD AKA TOTE ROAD

N.F.S GRATE

PRIVATE DOCK

MOOSE

BEAR

DEER

NORTH FORK OF WICKI UP CRK.

"STOCKADE ISLAND

VIRGIN WHITE PINE STAND

THE NARROWS (N)

MOCCASIN BAY

WALLEYES SPAWNING AREA

FALLEN
COOK COU
960 ACRE-
MAXIMUM
NEAREST to
RESIDENT FIS
WALLEYE PIKE
GREAT NORTHER
YELLOW PERCH
TIGER MUSKEL
PUMPKIN SEED
BROWN SUCKER
WHITE SUCKER
TULLIBEE